MAKING IT
TO HEAVEN

How to Be Certain You'll
Spend Eternity with God

John R. Lewis

Making It to Heaven
John R. Lewis

A.M.L. Publishing
New Glarus, WI

Library of Congress Control Number: 2014940885

ISBN: 978-1-940243-33-7

Unless otherwise indicated, all Scripture quotations designated (NIV) are taken from THE HOLY BIBLE, NEW INTERNATIONAL VERSION®, NIV® Copyright© 1973, 1978, 1984, 2011 by Biblica, Inc.® Used by permission. All rights reserved worldwide.

Quotations designated (NIV1984) are from THE HOLY BIBLE: NEW INTERNATIONAL VERSION®. NIV®. Copyright © 1973, 1978, 1984 by Biblica. All rights reserved worldwide.

Bold type or italics in Scripture quotations reflect the author's added emphasis.

ACKNOWLEDGMENTS

I would like to thank my wife, Angie Lewis, my mother, Susan Quinn, my pastor, Roger Olsen, and my friends, Michael Beil and Tony Gardner, for their help and input on this book.

I would also like to give special thanks to Ray Comfort and D. James Kennedy for their influence on my life and on this book. And a great thank you to Jesus Christ for saving me and giving me a new life!

TABLE OF CONTENTS

Chapter 1: Many Will Not Make It   1

Chapter 2: What Went Wrong?   11

Chapter 3: The Seriousness of Sin   23

Chapter 4: The Will of the Father   35

Chapter 5: Responding with Repentance   53

Chapter 6: How Can I Be Certain?   63

Chapter 7: Steps for Growth   75

Chapter 1

MANY WILL NOT MAKE IT

In the winter of 1993, while I was studying for my master's degree at Northern Michigan University, God brought some people into my life who began to ask me some heart-searching and life-changing questions; questions that would help lead me to be certain that I would make it to heaven when I died. One of those questions was this: "John, if you died today, are you 100 percent certain you would go to heaven?" Now, as far back as I can remember I had always assumed I would go to heaven because I believed in God, tried to go to church every Sunday, and because I was a pretty good person. I knew I wasn't perfect, but I never killed anybody or did anything real serious like that. However, this question made me stop and think, because although I thought I would go to heaven, I couldn't actually say that I was 100 percent certain I would go there when I died. I didn't even know it was possible to know this before one died.

You Can Be Certain

All of my life I thought that you would find out where you will spend eternity after you die. I was then shown a verse from the Bible that would change my thinking about this. It was written by John, one of the apostles of Jesus Christ, and says, **"I write these things to you . . . so that you may *know* that you *have* eternal life"** (1 John 5:13). I was shown from this verse that one of the reasons the Bible was written was so that we might *know* for certain we *have* eternal life, which the Bible speaks of as eternity in heaven. This scripture verse says that the certainty of making it to heaven is something we can have now—present tense. We don't have to wait until we die to find out if we will make it to heaven. In other words, you don't have to just hope you will make it to heaven someday; you can actually know today and be 100 percent certain you will go there when you die. So let me ask you that same question that was asked of me many years ago: If you died today, are you 100 percent certain you would go to heaven? YES or NO (please circle one).

A Serious Matter

Most people today don't think too much about death, the afterlife, or where they will spend eternity. At least not until they get a life-threatening disease, have a close call in an accident, or a close friend or family member dies (and for most of us, these things don't happen very often). Most of us believe that we will have many more years to live and that death is something that seems to happen to other people, not us. But if we are all honest, we would have to admit that today could be our last day. Over 150,000 people die every day! I'm sure most of the 150,000 people who died yesterday didn't wake up thinking it would be their last day on earth. You see, no one is promised another day—not even another minute . . . or breath, for that matter. I know that death is not a fun thing to think about, but it does us good to think about it because it causes us to live life differently and take the matter of where we will spend eternity more seriously. There is nothing more serious in this life to consider than where we will spend eternity. After all, eternity is forever!

Here on earth, both our thoughts and lives are very busy with many different things. However, in light of the possible nearness of death and the length and seriousness of eternity, shouldn't we stop and take some time to think about our own death and specifically, where we will spend eternity? Since there is nothing more important than where you will spend eternity, nothing is more important for you right now than learning how to make it to heaven and being 100 percent certain you will go there when you die. If you don't yet have this certainty of making it to heaven, you are missing out on something that God wants you to have. It is something that will bring you great peace and joy because it will help take away the fear of death and what happens afterward. So please, continue reading and let me help you discover this for your own life.

"There is nothing more serious in this life to consider than where we will spend eternity. After all, eternity is forever!"

Many Are Turned Away

You do not want to guess at or assume where you will spend eternity as I did for so many years. It's not something you can afford to be wrong about. Can you imagine going your whole life thinking you will make it into heaven, then after dying, finding out you were wrong, and end up spending eternity in hell? Talk about a rude awakening! That would be horrible! But Jesus Christ Himself said this would happen to *many* people. Look at His words in Matthew 7:21-23: **"Not everyone who says to me, 'Lord, Lord,' will enter the kingdom of heaven, but only the one who does the will of my Father who is in heaven. Many will say to me on that day, 'Lord, Lord, did we not prophesy in your name and in your name drive out demons and in your name perform many miracles?' Then I will tell them plainly, 'I never knew you. Away from me, you evildoers!'"**

Here is a quick look at these people who didn't make it into heaven.

- They believed in Jesus. They even called Him Lord.

- They did some amazing works for Him. They prophesied (spoke) in His name, drove out demons, and did many miracles. Surely this group of people should have made it into heaven, right? Yet we see that on their Judgment Day, Jesus claims He never knew them and sends them away, calling them "evildoers."

- These people expected they would make it into heaven, yet they were turned away and would now have to spend all of eternity in hell.

The frightening thing is that Jesus said this would happen to *many* people, not just a few. A few verses earlier, in Matthew 7:13-14, Jesus talked about the *many* people who won't make it into heaven, saying: **"Enter through the narrow gate. For wide is the gate and broad is the road that leads to destruction, and *many* enter through it. But small is the gate and narrow the road that leads to life, and only a *few* find it."** Jesus is saying here that *many* will take the road that leads to destruction, or hell, and by comparison, only a *few* will take the road that leads to life, which is heaven.

Hell Is a Real Place

It is sad to think that there will be more people in hell than there will be in heaven, but Jesus Himself said this would be the case. There are some who think that God will let everyone into heaven, but this is not true. Jesus said, **"*Not everyone* who says to me, 'Lord, Lord' will enter the kingdom of heaven"** (Matthew 7:21). Hell is a real place and Jesus spoke about it quite often. In fact, He spoke about hell more often than He did about heaven. If we believe in the heaven that Jesus spoke of, we must also believe in the hell He spoke of too.

"Hell is a real place and Jesus spoke about it quite often. In fact, He spoke about hell more often than He did about heaven."

We hear a lot these days about people who have died, gone to heaven, and come back to life to tell us many wonderful things about heaven. However, there are also many real-life documentaries and books written about people who died, went to hell, and came back to tell about the reality and horrors of it. These stories don't seem to make the headlines or talk show circuits like the stories of those who have been to heaven. I personally know two people who died, went to heaven, walked and talked with Jesus, and then came back to life to tell about it. I also know of people who have gone to hell and back, and their stories are quite frightening. Hell is not a fun place to go, where people will party with their friends. The Bible describes hell as **"the blazing furnace, where there will be weeping and gnashing of teeth"** (Matthew 13:50), and a place where **"the worms that eat them do not die, and the fire is not quenched"** (Mark 9:48).

What About Purgatory?

You may be wondering about or putting your hope in purgatory, the place some believe they will go after death if they weren't quite bad enough to go to hell, yet not quite good enough to enter heaven. In purgatory, they believe they will be able to improve their spiritual status before God through suffering, or by the prayers and intercession of others. However, neither Jesus nor the apostles ever spoke of purgatory, and nowhere is it found in the Bible. Purgatory was fabricated by Pope Innocent IV, in a letter to the apostolic delegates in Greece, March 6, 1254, twelve centuries after the death of Jesus and His apostles. The Bible makes it very clear that there is no such place as purgatory. In fact, Hebrews 9:27 says, **"people are destined to die once, and after that to face judgment."** So after our death, there will be no time or place for improving ourselves, no chance to do things over or make things right. There will be judgment, and then there will be either heaven or hell for all eternity.

Help with Doubts

You may be reading this and thinking, *I'm not sure if I believe in God*, or *I'm not sure if I believe in the Bible*. We must first realize that our beliefs don't determine truth or reality. Just because I don't believe in something doesn't mean it's not true or doesn't exist. If I don't believe in gravity and step off a ten-story building, I'm going to fall to my death whether I believe in gravity or not. God doesn't exist because I believe He does, and if I don't believe He exists, it doesn't make Him disappear. Likewise, the Bible is the inspired Word of God, not because I believe it is, but because God says it is and there is much evidence to prove this is true. The main purpose of this book is not to prove to you the existence of God or that the Bible is the inspired Word of God. There are plenty of books out there that do a great job of proving these things. However, if you are struggling with these issues, the next few paragraphs will give you a few things to think about.

Creation Points to a Creator

God does exist and He has revealed Himself to all mankind in many ways. One of the ways we know that God exists is through the world around us. The Bible says in Romans 1:18-20, **"The wrath of God is being revealed from heaven against all the godlessness and wickedness of people, who suppress the truth by their wickedness, since what may be known about God is *plain* to them, because God has made it *plain* to them. For since the creation of the world God's invisible qualities—his eternal power and divine nature—have** been *clearly seen, being understood from what has been made,* **so that people are without excuse.**" This verse says that God has made His existence *plain* to all mankind and that it can be *clearly seen* and *understood* from all that He has made, so nobody has an excuse for not knowing God exists. Psalm 19:1-4 (NIV 1984) says, **"The heavens declare the glory of God; the skies proclaim the work of his hands. Day after day they pour forth speech; night after night they display knowledge. There is no speech or language where their voice is not heard. Their voice goes out into all the earth, their words to the ends of the world."** This means that every day, God's creation is speaking to all of mankind all over the world, telling us He does exist. It says here that what we see in the sky gives us the knowledge that He is real and that He created all that we see.

If you look at the amazing beauty and details of space, with all the planets and stars, our own Sun and Moon, there is order, purpose, and design. If you look at our own planet, Earth, and all the amazing creatures that fill the land, air, and sea, there is order, purpose, and design. If you look at the amazing human body, there is order, purpose, and design. All of these things couldn't possibly have happened by accident, by evolution, or by a "big bang." Explosions don't create order and beauty; they cause disorder, chaos, and destruction. Consider for a moment the design and complexity of your cell phone, computer, or car, and all that they can do. You would never imagine even the possibility that any of them could have come together by accident. You know they must have been created by someone with great intelligence. How then can we look at the world around us and the human body and think that there is no Creator, that it all came about by accident or through evolution? The human body can do infinitely more than a cell phone, car, or computer, and is much more complex; revealing that there has to be a Creator. The design and complexity of the human eye alone is enough to prove there had to be a Creator.

Charles Darwin, father of evolutionary theory, had this to say about the human eye: "To suppose that the eye, with all its inimitable contrivances for adjusting the focus to different distances, for admitting different amounts of light, and for the correction of spherical and chromatic aberration, could have formed by natural selection, seems, I freely confess, absurd in the highest degree."[1] Evolutionist Robert Jastrow had this to say about the human eye: "The eye appears to have been designed; no designer of telescopes could have done better. How could this marvelous instrument have evolved by chance, through a succession of random events? Many people in Darwin's day agreed with theologian William Pauley, who commented, 'There cannot be a design without a designer.'"[2]

The reason many people can't seem to find God is because they aren't seriously looking for Him. In fact, many are actually running from Him. God says in His Word, **"You will seek me and find me when you seek me with all your heart"** (Jeremiah 29:13). So if you want to find God and know that He exists, just seek Him with all your heart. If you aren't sure He exists yet, maybe it's because you haven't looked for Him with all your heart.

Merely believing in God's existence isn't enough to get you into heaven though. The Bible says in James 2:19, **"You believe that there is one God. Good! Even the demons believe that— and shudder."** James is saying here that believing in God's existence isn't really a big deal, even the demons of hell believe that. If believing in God's existence was enough to get someone into heaven, then even the demons would be there.

God Wrote the Bible

God has also made Himself known through the Bible, also called the Word of God, or the Scripture. Some people don't believe the Bible because they think it is just the thoughts and words of men, but they have never taken the time to examine the Bible for themselves. The Bible itself claims to be the actual words of

God Himself, written down by men. Think about it this way: When you write a letter, who is doing the writing, you or the pen? You are doing the writing; the pen is just the instrument you are using to communicate your thoughts. Similarly, God wrote the Bible; men were just the instruments He chose to communicate His thoughts to us. The Bible says, **"All Scripture is God-breathed"** (2 Timothy 3:16). This means that all the words in the Bible were inspired by God, or "breathed" out of His mouth, which were then written down by men. The Bible is an incredible book. There is no other book like it. It is the number one best seller of all time for a reason—it is the inspired Word of God!

The Evidence of Prophecy

There is much evidence to prove the Bible is the inspired Word of God, one of those being the thousands of prophesies it contains. There are approximately 3,856 verses directly or indirectly containing prophecy in the Bible. These predictions are not general or vague; they are very specific, detailed, and contain information that could not have been known to people unless God Himself had revealed it to them. Some two thousand specific prophecies have been fulfilled, and many are being fulfilled today before our very eyes. If you look at any other religious books or writings in the world today—the writings of the Hindus, Buddhists, Muslims, or any others—you will see that none of them contain predictive prophecies like the Bible does. The Bible stands apart from all others and is the only one that actually claims and proves to be the inspired Word of God. The many fulfilled prophecies of the Bible are just one proof that the words in the Bible come from God Himself, not man.

God knew that men would have disputes about what is true and what to believe, so He gave us something firm and solid to stand upon, His Word. The Bible is the Word of God and it is where we must look for truth and for what to believe. We must not rely on the words or traditions of men or our religious denomination.

The Bible has been proven to be trustworthy, accurate, and true, and has remained the same for thousands of years. Over that time, many have tried to destroy or disprove the Bible, without success. In fact, no one has succeeded in disproving even one point of what the Bible says.

> **"The many fulfilled prophecies of the Bible are just one proof that the words in the Bible come from God Himself, not man."**

Further Help

There are many other facts that prove God's existence and that the Bible is His inspired words. But as I mentioned earlier, the purpose of this book is not to prove the existence of God or to prove that the Bible is the inspired Word of God. There are plenty of books out there on these subjects. However, if you need further help with any doubts or questions, I suggest that you seek out such books and study these things for yourself. I highly recommend two books by Ray Comfort that focus on proving the existence of God: *God Doesn't Believe in Atheists* and, *How to Know God Exists*. I also recommend two other books that will help you with any doubts or questions you may have about the Bible, they are written by Josh McDowell: *More Than a Carpenter*, and *The New Evidence that Demands a Verdict*. If you are serious about finding answers to your doubts or questions, these books will be a great help to you.

The Main Purpose

The main purpose of this book is to show people—from the Word of God—how they can make it to heaven and be 100 percent certain they will go there when they die. Think again of the *many* people who expected to enter heaven but were ultimately turned away. What did they do wrong? Why couldn't they enter heaven? That is exactly what we will explore in the next chapter.

Chapter 2

WHAT WENT WRONG?

In the previous chapter we saw Jesus reveal that many people who expect to enter heaven will be turned away. Let's take a look at that passage of Scripture in Matthew 7 again: **"Not everyone who says to me, 'Lord, Lord,' will enter the kingdom of heaven, but only the one who does the will of my Father who is in heaven. Many will say to me on that day, 'Lord, Lord, did we not prophesy in your name and in your name drive out demons and in your name perform many miracles?' Then I will tell them plainly, 'I never knew you. Away from me, you evildoers!'"** (Matthew 7:21-23). Again, this description is of a great many people who believed in Jesus, called Him Lord, and did some amazing things in His name. So what went wrong? Why couldn't they enter heaven? It would be good for us to know this so we don't make the same mistake and miss entering heaven ourselves. Let's do all we can to make sure we don't find ourselves among the many who expect to enter heaven only to find out they were wrong. We wouldn't want that to happen to us or one of our family members, friends— anyone for that matter. Let's take a look and find out what went wrong.

There are two main reasons why these many people didn't make it into heaven, both of them are revealed in the passage of Scripture we just read above. First, notice that Jesus says, **"only the one who does *the will of my Father*"** (Matthew 7:21), will enter the kingdom of heaven. These many people couldn't enter heaven because they didn't do *the will of the Father.* If they had, they would have entered. In other words, they didn't do what God required of them to enter heaven. So what does God require of us to enter heaven? What do we have to do? How good do we have to be? What is *the will of the Father* that Jesus is talking about that we must do to enter heaven? That's what we will explore in coming chapters.

Another Important Question

Before we get into that, I have to ask you another very important question. Your answer to this question will actually reveal whether or not you will make it into heaven—that's how important it is. This question is one of those I mentioned in the beginning—one that radically changed my life and helped lead me to know that I would make it to heaven. The question is this: If you died today and stood before Jesus, and He asked you, "Why should I let you into heaven?" What would you say? Your answer to this question is so important that I am going to ask you to write it down in the space below or on a separate piece of paper. So please answer the question. Write down why you think Jesus should let you into heaven:

Did you write down your answer? If not, please go back and do so because the rest of this book will not be as meaningful if you don't, and you might miss truly understanding how to make it into heaven. Now, it is very important here for you to see and understand that your answer to that question reveals what you are *relying on* to enter heaven. It is very important for you to understand this, because *what you are relying on is the determining factor of whether or not you make it into heaven.* We will look at and deal with the significance of your answer at the end of this chapter, and in chapter four.

When I was originally asked that question over twenty years ago, I thought Jesus should let me into heaven because I believed in God, tried to go to church every Sunday, and because I was a pretty good person. That summed up what I was relying on to enter heaven someday. The big question is this: Is this what it takes to enter heaven? Is this *the will of the Father* that Jesus was talking about? I sure thought so. For most of my life that is what I was hoping would get me into heaven, but I soon found out I was very wrong. Believing in God, going to church, and being a good person are not what it takes to enter heaven. Where had I gone wrong? Where do so many go wrong in this matter? I will respond to this shortly, but for a moment, let's go back and look at our group of many people who missed entering heaven and find out what their answer to this question would have been, because *their answer reveals the other reason why they couldn't enter heaven.*

Their answer to this question is revealed in what they said to Jesus. Recall their words to Him in Matthew 7:22: **"Lord, Lord, did we not prophesy in your name and in your name drive out demons and in your name perform many miracles?"** These many people thought Jesus should let them into heaven because of the good things they had done for Him. They thought they were good enough to enter because they had prophesied, driven out demons, and performed many miracles. This is what they were *relying on* to enter heaven, and *because of that they could not enter.* Remember, what you are relying on is *the* determining factor of whether or not you make it into heaven. They had hoped that by their own goodness, good deeds, and religious works, they could earn their way into heaven. *The Bible makes it very clear that no one will enter heaven by trying to be a good person, by doing good things, or by any religious works. Anyone who is relying on these types of things will not make it to heaven.* This is the other reason these many people didn't make it to heaven. The first reason they missed entering heaven was because they didn't do *the will of the Father* (exactly what this is will be revealed in chapter four). The second reason they missed entering heaven was because they were relying on the wrong thing to enter.

"The Bible makes it very clear that no one will enter heaven by trying to be a good person, by doing good things, or by any religious works."

There are many different keys on my keychain, but only one will unlock the door to my house. If I rely on the wrong key to enter my house, I'm not getting in, no matter how hard I try. These many people were relying on the wrong "key" to enter heaven, and therefore they couldn't get in.

We will spend the rest of this chapter and the next two revealing why no one will enter heaven by trying to be a good person, doing good things, or by any religious works.

God's Standard of Goodness

The majority of people in the world today are just like these many people. They believe they will be able to enter heaven because they have done good things in life—at least more good than bad—and because they consider themselves to be good people, not perfect, but no worse than the average person in the world today. This is what most people are relying on and hope will get them into heaven someday. But how good do you have to be? What is God's standard of goodness to enter by which we can measure ourselves? The answer is revealed in a conversation Jesus had with a rich ruler found in Luke 18:18-23 (NIV1984):

> A certain ruler asked him, "Good teacher, what must I do to inherit eternal life?" "Why do you call me good?" Jesus answered. "No one is good—except God alone.

You know the commandments: 'Do not commit adultery, do not murder, do not steal, do not give false testimony, honor your father and mother.'" "All these I have kept since I was a boy," he said. When Jesus heard this, he said to him, "You still lack one thing. Sell everything you have and give to the poor, and you will have treasure in heaven. Then come, follow me." When he heard this, he became very sad, because he was a man of great wealth."

When this rich man asked Jesus what he had to do to inherit eternal life, or enter the kingdom of heaven, Jesus first corrected the man's understanding of "good" by telling him that, **"*No one is good*—except God alone"** (Luke 18:19). Jesus said this because God's definition of *good* is being perfect in thought, word, and deed, and only God is that good. Then Jesus gave him five of the Ten Commandments, the ones that had to do with his fellow man. The Ten Commandments reveal God's standard of goodness. When the man claimed he had kept the five commandments Jesus mentioned, Jesus told him to sell everything he had and give it to the poor and then come and follow Him.

". . . God's definition of *good* is being perfect in thought, word, and deed, and only God is that good."

Why did Jesus say these things to the rich man? Is this what it takes to enter heaven? Can we become good enough to enter heaven by trying to obey the Ten Commandments? Can we earn our way into heaven by our good works, like selling everything we have and giving it to the poor? The answer is no. As we mentioned earlier, no one will enter heaven by trying to be a good person or by their good works. But then why did Jesus say these things to the rich man if they wouldn't get him into heaven?

The Purpose of God's Law

To truly understand why Jesus said what He did and what He was trying to accomplish with the rich man, we must first understand the true purpose of the Ten Commandments, which are also referred to as God's Law. Their true purpose is revealed by the apostle Paul in Romans 3:20 (NIV1984): **"Therefore no one will be declared righteous in his sight by observing the law; rather, through the law we become conscious of sin."** The apostle Paul is saying two things here. First, he is saying that no one will be declared righteous or *good* in God's eyes by trying to obey God's Law, because no one can perfectly obey it. Secondly, he is saying the real purpose of God's Law is to make us conscious or aware of our sin. The Ten Commandments were never given to us as a means of trying to be good enough to enter heaven, but to reveal that we are not good; that we have sinned against a holy God and are in need of His mercy and forgiveness. This is exactly why Jesus said what He did and what He was trying to reveal to the rich man.

"The Ten Commandments were never given to us as a means of trying to be good enough to enter heaven, but to reveal that we are not good;"

This rich man thought he was good, which is revealed in his claim that he had kept all the commandments Jesus listed. At the beginning of their conversation Jesus came right out and told him that he wasn't good by saying, **"*No one is good*—Except God alone"** (Luke 18:19). Next Jesus gave him five of the Ten Commandments to help him see that he wasn't good; that he had sinned against God, and because of this, *there was nothing he could do to earn his way into heaven*—he needed God's mercy and forgiveness. This didn't work with the rich man because he thought he had kept the five commandments Jesus mentioned. We will see very soon that this man did not perfectly keep these commandments, nor has anyone else. Jesus then said to him, **"You still lack**

one thing" (Luke 18:22). What he lacked was an awareness of his sin. Jesus now had to hit him where it would hurt, where his sin would be the most obvious—his love of money. Jesus gave him a directive that would help him clearly see he had sinned against God and wasn't good because he had made money the "god" of his life. He had broken the first of the Ten Commandments, which says, **"You shall have no other gods before me"** (Exodus 20:3). We don't know what ultimately happened to this man, but we know that after Jesus told him to sell everything he had and give it to the poor, he became very sad.

Are You a Good Person?

Many people today, like the rich man, think they are good because they aren't aware of their sin or because they haven't compared themselves against God's standard of goodness revealed in the Ten Commandments. Most people tend to compare themselves with the rest of mankind. This is relative to those with whom we compare ourselves. If you compare yourself with Adolf Hitler or Jeffery Dahmer, you will probably look great, but if you compare yourself with Billy Graham or Mother Teresa, you may not look as good as you thought. Most people tend to compare themselves with the average person they see every day and seem to fare up about the same—not perfect, but pretty good.

But does God compare us against each other and then grade on a curve? No. God compares us to Himself and His standard of goodness, which again is revealed in His Law, the Ten Commandments.

The Ten Commandments act like a mirror. When we look into them we can see ourselves in truth, exactly how God see us. Take a look into the mirror of God's Law for just a moment to see how you look according to His standard. Start by looking at the commandments Jesus gave to the rich man: **"Do not commit adultery, do not murder, do not steal, do not give false testimony, honor your father and mother"** (Luke 18:20, NIV1984).

Adultery

Have you ever committed adultery—cheated on your spouse? Maybe not, but look at what Jesus said in Matthew 5:27-28 (NIV1984): **"You have heard that it was said, 'Do not commit adultery.' But I tell you that anyone who looks at a woman lustfully has already committed adultery with her in his heart."** God is so holy and perfect that He sees lust as adultery. Have you ever looked at someone with lust? Have you lusted by looking at pornography? Have romance novels or the shows you watch on TV or at the movies caused you to lust? Whether you are married or not, if you have ever looked at someone with lust, Jesus says you are guilty of committing adultery.

Murder

Have you ever murdered anyone? Probably not, but look at what God's Word says to us in 1 John 3:15, **"Anyone who hates a brother or sister *is* a murderer."** Again, God is so holy and perfect, He sees hatred as murder. Have you ever hated anyone? If you have, then by God's standard and judgment, you are a murderer. Regarding murder, Jesus also said this in Matthew 5:21-22: **"You have heard that it was said to the people long ago, 'You shall not murder, and anyone who murders will be subject to judgment.' But I tell you that anyone who is angry with a brother or sister will be subject to judgment."** Here Jesus is saying that unjust anger is on the same level as murder, deserving the same judgment. That's how holy God is and how high His standard is. Have you ever been unjustly angry at someone? If you have, Jesus says you are in the same category as someone who has committed murder.

Stealing

Have you ever stolen anything? In your entire life, have you ever taken something that did not belong to you, even something of little value? The value of the item taken doesn't matter. If we take something that doesn't belong to us, it is stealing and that makes us a thief in God's eyes. Most people, at least once in their lifetime, take something that doesn't belong to them, whether a piece of candy, some small change, or something from their workplace. Most of us, if not all, would be guilty of breaking this commandment and would therefore be thieves by God's judgment.

False Testimony (Lying)

Have you ever given false testimony (lied)? Who hasn't told a lie, right? In your entire life, how many lies do you think you've told? Hundreds? Thousands? It doesn't really matter, because telling even one lie makes us guilty of breaking this commandment and actually makes us liars. That may seem pretty harsh, but how many lies do we have to tell to become a liar? Ten and a bell goes off? No, even telling one lie makes us a liar.

Honoring Your Parents

Have you always, without fail, honored your father and mother? Have you always obeyed and respected your parents? There probably isn't a person alive who hasn't at one point in their life, in some way, dishonored their parents. So it would probably be safe to say that you would be guilty of breaking this commandment too.

So how did you do? If you are like the average person in the world today, you have probably broken most, if not all of these commandments. And just think, we've only looked at five of them. There are five more out there to look into and by which we can judge ourselves.

Blasphemy

The third commandment says, **"You shall not misuse the name of the Lord your God"** (Exodus 20:7). Have you ever misused God's name by saying, "Oh my G@#!"? Have you ever used the name of Jesus Christ as a swear word? This is blasphemy and is very serious in God's eyes. Psalm 139:20 says, **"They speak of you with evil intent; your adversaries misuse your name."** If we have misused God's name, we are seen as His adversaries or enemies—that's how serious this offense is to God.

Idolatry

The first commandment says, **"You shall have no other gods before me"** (Exodus 20:3). Has God always been first in your life? Have you ever been guilty of putting anything before God and made it the "god" of your life? The Bible calls this idolatry and if we have done this we become idolaters in God's eyes.

Conclusion

Well, I think that is probably enough of looking into the mirror of God's Law because it is somewhat painful to look at ourselves in this light and find out that we don't look so good after all. I hope that you have gotten the point of all this: So many people think they will be able to enter heaven because they think they are good people. They might be good according to the world's standard, but as we have seen, no one is good according to God's standard.

The conclusion of looking into the mirror of God's Law and comparing ourselves with His standard can be summed up in the following two verses:

> **For all have sinned and fall short of the glory of God.** (Romans 3:23)

> **All of us have become like one who is unclean, and all our righteous acts are like filthy rages; we all shrivel up like a leaf, and like the wind our sins sweep us away.** (Isaiah 64:6)

Romans 3:23 reveals that it's not man's standard of goodness that we are judged by and fall short on, but God's. It says that because of our sin we all fall short of God's glory, which is His perfect holiness. That's God's ultimate standard. Jesus said in Matthew 5:48, **"Be perfect, therefore, as your heavenly Father is perfect."** Compared to God's perfect holiness we are all unclean and our righteous acts, our good deeds, and the very best we can do and offer are like filthy rags in His sight. Imagine, if this is what our best looks like to God, what must our sin look like to Him?

". . . it's not man's standard of goodness that we are judged by and fall short on, but God's."

Like the rich man, this might make us sad, but to understand how to make it into heaven, we must first understand that we have sinned against a perfect and holy God and because of that we are not good by God's standard and, therefore, unable to enter heaven by relying on our own goodness or the good things we have done.

Remember the words of those many people as to why they thought Jesus should let them into heaven, **"Lord, Lord, did we not prophesy in your name and in your name drive out demons and in your name perform many miracles?"** (Matthew 7:22). They thought they were good and good enough to enter heaven because of the good things they had done for Jesus, and this is where they went wrong. Like most people today, they were relying on their own goodness, good deeds, and religious works to enter heaven. Because they were relying on these things, they could not enter heaven. Once again, the Bible makes it very clear that no one will enter heaven because of these things.

What Are You Relying On?

Take a moment and look back at your answer to our question at the beginning of the chapter. *Why do you think Jesus should let you into heaven?* What is it you are relying on to enter heaven? If it has anything to do with being a good person, doing good things, or any religious works, you will not be able to enter heaven. Again, anyone who is relying on their own goodness, good deeds, or religious works will not be able to enter heaven. This is *not* how we make it into to heaven. This is not *the will of the Father* that Jesus spoke of.

Well, if trying to be a good person and doing good deeds or religious works doesn't get us into heaven, then what does? What is *the will of the Father* that Jesus spoke of that we must do to enter the kingdom of heaven? I can't wait to tell you, but not yet. To truly understand how to make it into heaven, we must first understand the seriousness of our sins before God and their consequences. We will deal with this in the next chapter.

Chapter 3

THE SERIOUSNESS OF SIN

Many people today have the mindset that most of their sin isn't really a big deal. Everyone would probably agree that things like rape, murder, adultery, and armed robbery are serious sins, but many think lightly of things like lying, stealing, swearing, dishonoring their parents, sex before marriage, pornography, drunkenness, and more. Most people don't consider these kinds of sins to be a big deal compared to things like rape and murder because "everyone is doing them" and most of them seem to come naturally to us. Who hasn't told a lie? Who hasn't stolen something small? Who hasn't cursed or misused God's name? Who hasn't disobeyed or dishonored his or her parents? Who hasn't had sex before getting married? Who hasn't looked at pornography? Who hasn't gotten drunk? We don't take these kinds of sins serious because they are so common and all around us every day.

Another reason many people don't think too much of these "common" sins is because there doesn't seem to be any serious consequences to them. After all, most of these things aren't going to land one in jail. Many of us have the belief that if it doesn't land us in jail it must not be that serious to God either. We also think that if God doesn't instantly punish us or strike us dead, He must be okay with what we are doing, or it must not be that serious in His eyes.

These ways of thinking are very far from the truth of what the Bible reveals about the seriousness of sin and how God views and deals with it. Just because "everyone" does something and it seems to come naturally to us does not mean God is okay with it. Just because it doesn't land you in jail or God doesn't punish you right away does not mean that it's not a serious thing before God. In this chapter, we will take a look at the seriousness of sin in God's eyes and its dire consequences.

In the Beginning

To understand the seriousness of our sin and its consequences, we need to go back to the beginning, when God first created mankind. In the first book of the Bible, Genesis, we can see that God created everything absolutely perfect, and when He was done creating everything, it says, **"God saw all that he had made, and it was very good"** (Genesis 1:31). So in the very beginning, mankind was created sinless and made perfect by God; but this would soon change.

". . . in the very beginning, mankind was created sinless and made perfect by God; but this would soon change."

The story of mankind's fall into sin and its consequences is found in the book of Genesis, chapters 2 and 3. The Bible says: **"The Lord God took the man and put him in the Garden of Eden to work it and take care of it. And the Lord God commanded the man, 'You are free to eat from any tree in the garden; but you must not eat from the tree of the knowledge of good and evil, *for when you eat from it you will certainly die'"* (Genesis 2:15-17). The story continues as we see Satan speaking to Eve through a serpent and tempting her to eat from the forbidden tree. The Bible says: **"When the woman saw that the fruit of the tree was good for food and pleasing** to the eye, and also desirable for gaining wisdom, she took some and ate it. She also gave some to her husband, who was with her, and he ate it" (Genesis 3:6).

What was the big deal about eating a piece of fruit and what were the consequences? In God's eyes, this was a big deal. They had disobeyed His command and sinned against Him— mankind's first sin. Remember what God had said earlier about eating the fruit: **"for when you eat from it you will certainly die"** (Genesis 2:17). God said the consequence of this sin would be death!

Spiritual Death

When Adam and Eve ate the fruit they didn't physically die. Was God lying? No. God was not lying. A death did happen that day. It was not a physical death, it was a spiritual death. To understand this concept of spiritual death, we must see death in terms of a *separation* that takes place, rather than something that ceases to exist.

Think about it. When you die physically, you don't cease to exist. Rather, the real you—your spirit—is just separated from your body, though still very much alive. So when Adam and Eve sinned against God, they died spiritually, meaning, *they were now separated from God*; their relationship with God was dead! This spiritual death, or separation from God, has been passed down to every human since Adam and Eve. The Bible makes this clear in Romans 5:12: **"Therefore, just as sin entered the world through one man, and death through sin, and in this way death came to all people, because all sinned."** By their sin, Adam and Eve brought onto all mankind both spiritual and physical death.

We may think this is unfair, point the finger, and put the blame on Adam and Eve, but it's clear that we have all chosen to sin and disobey God in many ways ourselves. So the very first consequence to mankind's sin is that we are all born *spiritually dead* and *separated from God*. The Bible makes this clear over and over again with scriptures such as Ephesians 2:1, **"As for you, you were *dead* in your transgressions and sins,"** and Isaiah 59:2, **"But your iniquities have *separated* you from your God."** This concept of spiritual death helps us to understand the statement that Jesus made in John 3:3 (NIV1984): **"I tell you the truth, no one can see the kingdom of God unless he is *born again*."** Jesus is saying here that unless we are spiritually *reborn* (born again) we cannot enter the kingdom of God. In other words, unless we are spiritually *reunited* with God *before we die*, we will spend eternity *separated* from Him. The state of our relationship with God at our death will determine where we will spend eternity. If we are still separated from Him at our death, we will spend eternity separated from Him in hell. If we have been reunited with Him before we die, we will spend eternity united with Him in heaven. If Jesus said we can't enter heaven unless we are *born again*, wouldn't it be wise for us to find out *how* we can be *born again*? Well, this is part of what happens to you when you do *the will of the Father* that Jesus spoke about in Matthew 7:21. This will finally be revealed in the next chapter.

"If Jesus said we can't enter heaven unless we are *born again*, wouldn't it be wise for us to find out *how* we can be *born again*?"

Frightening Consequences

To further understand the serious nature of our sin and its consequences, here are some scriptures that list specific sins and their frightening consequences:

> **Do you not know that the wicked *will not inherit the kingdom of God?* Do not be deceived: Neither the sexually immoral nor idolaters nor adulterers nor male prostitutes nor homosexual offenders nor thieves nor the greedy nor drunkards nor slanderers nor swindlers**

will inherit the kingdom of God. (1 Corinthians 6:9-10, NIV1984)

The acts of the flesh are obvious: sexual immorality, impurity and debauchery; idolatry and witchcraft; hatred, discord, jealousy, fits of rage, selfish ambition, dissensions, factions and envy; drunkenness, orgies, and the like. I warn you, as I did before, that those who live like this *will not inherit the kingdom of God.* (Galatians 5:19-21)

But the cowardly, the unbelieving, the vile, the murderers, the sexually immoral, those who practice magic arts, the idolaters and all liars—*they will be consigned to the fiery lake of burning sulfur.* (Revelation 21:8)

The consequence to the sins listed above is that those who are involved in them will not inherit the kingdom of God, meaning they will not make it to heaven but, **"they will be consigned to the fiery lake of burning sulfur"** (Revelation 21:8), which is hell.

Am I Guilty?

Now you have to ask yourself: *Am I guilty of any of the sins listed above?* As you look at the sins mentioned above, remember from the previous chapter that if you have ever looked at another with lust, you are considered by God to be an *adulterer*; if you hated someone or had unjust anger, you are a *murderer* in God's eyes; if you have ever stolen anything, regardless of the value of the item taken, you are a *thief*; if you have ever told a lie, even once, you are a *liar*. Are you guilty of any of these sins? If so, then according to the scriptures we just looked at you will not be able to enter the kingdom of heaven. This is the serious and eternal consequence of our sin!

These scriptures also say that those who are *sexually immoral* will also be excluded from entering the kingdom of heaven. This not only includes adultery, but also things like rape, incest, child molestation, and sex before marriage. Are you guilty of having sex before marriage? Though this is very common in our day and most people don't think it is a very big deal, the Bible calls this sexual immorality, and those who are sexually immoral will not be allowed into the kingdom of heaven. I used to think that sex before marriage wasn't a big deal. Then I saw the verses shown above and I realized that I was in big trouble. I was literally headed for hell.

What about *drunkenness*? Is getting drunk a regular habit for you? I always thought that getting drunk wasn't a big deal. It seemed fun and natural and everyone was doing it, but I never really knew what God thought about it until I read the Bible. He says in these verses that those who practice drunkenness cannot enter the kingdom of heaven. Are you guilty of this sin? If so, then you cannot enter heaven.

These verses also say that *idolaters* will not inherit the kingdom of God. Idolatry is worshipping something other than the one true God. This would include putting anything before God in your life, or worshipping a God you create in your own mind (one who is different from the God revealed in Scripture). Many people do this without even realizing it. When people say things like, "My God is a God of love and He would never send anyone to hell," they are committing idolatry by worshipping a God they have created in their own minds. However, they are right; their "God" would never send anyone to hell, because he cannot—he doesn't exist. Their "God" is a figment of their own imagination, an act of idolatry.

Have you ever committed idolatry by putting something before God in your life, or by creating a God in your own mind; one who is different from the God revealed in the Scriptures, one with whom you are more comfortable, who is okay with certain sins in your life? If you have done this, the Bible says you are an *idolater*, and idolaters cannot enter the kingdom of heaven.

I think the most frightening indictment in this list of scriptures is the statement: **"*all liars*—they will be consigned to**

the fiery lake of burning sulfur" (Revelation 21:8). From this verse, it looks like we are all headed for hell! After all, who hasn't told at least one lie in his or her entire life? Some may think this seems harsh, "just for lying," but this is because we are fallen, sinful humans, and we don't see sin the same way a perfect and holy God does. The Bible reveals that all sin is a serious offense against God, but lying is listed as a sin that God *hates*.

The book of Proverbs, chapter six, lists some of the sins that God hates and are detestable to Him. Among them are, **"a lying tongue,"** (Proverbs 6:17), and **"a false witness who pours out lies"** (Proverbs 6:19). Lying is so detestable to God that in the book of Acts, chapter five, He actually killed a husband and wife, Ananias and Sapphira, for telling one lie! That's how serious lying is to God. Our reaction to this should not be: "God, why did you kill them for just telling one lie?" Our reaction should be: "God, why didn't you kill me the last time I told a lie?" The reason He didn't is because He chose to show you mercy and not give you what your sins deserve.

To understand the serious nature of sin in God's eyes, think about this for a moment: When you listen to the news and hear that someone has been given a death sentence or life sentence for the crimes they committed, you can assume that what they did must have been pretty horrendous. However, if you hear of someone having to pay a $100 fine, you can conclude that the crime they committed must not have been too bad. The seriousness of the crime is equated to the punishment. If someone's punishment is eternity in hell—the fiery lake of burning sulfur—you can conclude that what they have done must have been very evil and wicked in the eyes of the judge.

No Sin Allowed

On Judgment Day Jesus Christ will be our judge and in His eyes all sin is evil and very wicked. Because He is absolutely holy, pure, and perfect, no sin will be allowed into His eternal kingdom. The

Bible makes this clear in Psalm 5:4 (NIV1984): **"You are not a God who takes pleasure in evil; with you the wicked cannot dwell."** Also, Habakkuk 1:13 says, **"Your eyes are too pure to look on evil; you cannot tolerate wrongdoing."** In the book of Revelation, the apostle John talks about the kingdom of heaven and says, **"Nothing impure will ever enter it, nor will anyone who does what is shameful or deceitful"** (Revelation 21:27). This means that on Judgment Day, anyone who is found with even one sin on their record will be found guilty and will not be allowed into the kingdom of heaven.

". . . on Judgment Day, anyone who is found with even one sin on their record will be found guilty and will not be allowed into the kingdom of heaven."

James 2:10 confirms that it takes only one sin to make us guilty before God: **"For whoever keeps the whole law and yet stumbles at just *one point* is guilty of breaking all of it."** But who of us has sinned only once? In thought, word, or deed, most of us sin hundreds of times in the course of a day. Imagine if you were good enough to sin only five times a day. That would be 1,825 sins a year. If you lived to the age of seventy, that would be 127,000 sins on your record!

False Hopes

There are many things that people hope will help them with their sin on Judgment Day, but they are only false hopes and will not help them at all. Let's take a quick look at some of these false hopes and reveal their error.

Baptism. Some believe that baptism washes away their sins, but the Bible makes it clear that baptism does not wash away any sin—not even *original* sin, passed on from Adam and Eve. Baptism was never intended to wash away sin; this was never its purpose. (We will explore the true purpose of baptism later in this book.)

We need to remember that we must look to God's Word for our beliefs and practices, not the traditions of men or our church denomination. Being baptized is not going to help you with your sin on Judgment Day.

Confessing your sins. Some people think they will be okay on Judgment Day because they confess their sins to God or to a priest. First of all, the Bible makes it very clear that a priest cannot forgive sin, nor can any man, for that matter. The Scripture says that only God can forgive sin. However, simply confessing your sins to God isn't going to help you either. Try offering that plea in God's court-room: "Yes, Jesus, I committed all these sins, but I confessed them to you, so you should just forgive me and let me into heaven." To understand the error of this reasoning, think about how that plea would work in our earthly courtrooms. A man guilty of rape and murder stands before the judge and says: "Yes, judge, I am guilty. I confess that I raped and murdered that woman. However, because I confessed my crimes, I believe you should forgive me and let me go." Is the judge going to let him go just because he confessed his crimes? Of course not. If the judge is good and just, he will see that justice is done and the man is punished for his crimes. In the same way, just because we confess our sins to God doesn't mean that He is going to just forgive us and let us enter heaven. Justice must be done and our sins must be punished.

Time. Some people think that because they committed their sins a long time ago, somehow, they won't be held accountable for them. Today, many criminals are being tried and found guilty of crimes they committed twenty to thirty years ago. However, time doesn't erase their crime. It doesn't take away the fact that they did it and can still be caught and punished. Time will not take away our sins either or the justice and punishment that is due to us because of them.

Repentance. Some people put their hope in repentance or turning away from sin. Yes, Jesus commands us to turn from our sin, but this won't magically erase the sins we have committed or get us into heaven. Imagine this scenario in a court of law: "Judge, yes, I raped and murdered those women, but I have turned from my ways and I don't do those things anymore." Is the judge going to let him go just because he has stopped doing those things? Of course not. Similarly, our sins will not be forgiven just because we repent and stop doing them.

More good than bad. Another thing people put their hope in is that they believe they have done more good than bad. They believe that somehow they will balance the scales or tip them to their advantage by their good works. Picture someone trying that in a court of law: "Yes, judge, I stole that money, but I have done a lot of good things in my life—at least more good than bad." Is the judge going to let him go because of the good things he has done? Do his good works somehow magically erase the crime he has committed? No. Good works won't take away the guilt of his crime or the justice that must be done. And our good works won't take away our sins or help us on Judgment Day. Good works have no part in helping us get into heaven. Many times, they are an attempt to bribe the judge of the universe to let us into heaven, or to make up for all the sins we have committed.

God is loving and all-forgiving. Many people place their hope in the belief that God is so loving and forgiving that He is going to simply overlook and forgive all their sins, and let them into heaven. God is loving and forgiving, but He is also holy and just, and because of this, He must punish all sin. He will make sure perfect justice is accomplished on Judgment Day. Everyone with sin on their record will be sent to His eternal prison: hell.

"God is loving and forgiving, but He is also holy and just, and because of this, He must punish all sin."

God Wants No One in Hell

There are two very important things to remember about hell. First, it was not originally designed for humans. Matthew 25:41

says hell was **"prepared for the devil and his angels."** Second, it is not God's will or desire for any human to go there. First Timothy 2:4 says that God **"wants all people to be saved and come to a knowledge of the truth."** Second Peter 3:9 says, **"he is patient with you, not wanting anyone to perish."**

Summary Review

In the next chapter, we will finally reveal *the will of the Father* that Jesus spoke of in Matthew chapter 7, which is the only thing we can do to avoid hell and enter the kingdom of heaven. But before we reveal this, let's summarize what we have learned so far: We've learned that many people who expect to enter heaven will be turned away. These are people who believed in Jesus, called Him Lord, and did some amazing things for Him. We discovered that one of the reasons they missed entering heaven is because they didn't do *the will of the Father*. They didn't do what God required of them to enter. The other reason they couldn't enter heaven was because *they were relying on their own goodness, good deeds, and religious works to get in*. These things will not get us into heaven and anyone who relies on these things will not be able to enter. We discovered the reason these things can't get us into heaven is because we have all sinned against a holy God and no one is good, according to His perfect standard. We are all unclean before Him and the best we can do and offer is like a filthy rag in His sight. There is nothing we can do on our own to remove sin from our record or make up for the things we have done. We also discovered that our sin is a serious thing before God, and its consequences are separation from Him (spiritual death), not being able to inherit or enter the kingdom of heaven, and a deserved just punishment in hell.

This is terrible news for all of us. It should horrify us and cause us to have great concern about where we stand with God and where we will spend eternity. It should cause us to cry out like the jailer in Acts 16:30, **"What must I do to be saved?"** It should cause us to be desperate to read the next chapter so we can discover what *the will of the Father* is, for that alone can get us into heaven.

Chapter 4

THE WILL OF THE FATHER

Despite all the bad news and the seemingly hopeless predicament we have learned about in the last few chapters, there is hope and some good news to be shared. God, in His great love and mercy, has done something to save us from our sins and the hell we deserve. This good news is found in the person of Jesus Christ.

The good news is that about 2,000 years ago, God the Father sent God the Son, Jesus Christ, to earth. He was conceived supernaturally by God the Holy Spirit in a virgin named Mary. He was born sinless, untouched, and unaffected by the curse of sin, and He lived a sinless life. Hebrews 4:15 says this about Jesus, **"but we have one who has been tempted in every way, just as we are—yet was without sin"** (NIV1984). He was 100 percent man and 100 percent God. Though some people hold to the misconception that He was just a regular human, a son of God, He is called the "Son of God," a term of deity, meaning He was fully God.

Jesus Took Our Punishment

In the prime of His life, around the age of thirty-three, at the demand of the religious authorities of His day, Jesus was murdered by the Roman government by way of crucifixion for claiming to be God. Before they crucified the sinless God of the universe, they slapped Him in the face, punched Him in the face, and spat in His face. They mocked Him, put a crown of sharp, long thorns onto His head, and then hit him on the head again and again with a staff, driving the thorns into His head. If that wasn't bad enough, they whipped Him thirty-nine times, using leather strips with pieces of bone and metal on the end. This would have ripped open His back and penetrated to His organs. (The movie produced by Mel Gibson, *The Passion of the Christ*, offers a snapshot of all Christ endured, though the reality was far worse.)

"We have sinned against God by breaking His Laws, and Jesus stepped in and paid our fine in His own blood."

The Bible describes Jesus this way: **"his appearance was so disfigured beyond that of any human being and his form marred beyond human likeness"** (Isaiah 52:14). This means He was so beaten that He was not even recognizable as a human being. However, the Bible says **"it was the Lord's will to crush him and cause him to suffer"** (Isaiah 53:10). This was all being done according to God's predetermined plan because Jesus was taking upon Himself the punishment and wrath of God that was due to us because of our sin. It's as simple as this: We have sinned against God by breaking His Laws, and Jesus stepped in and paid our fine in His own blood. The Bible describes this clearly in the following scriptures:

> **But he was pierced for our transgressions, he was crushed for our iniquities; the punishment that brought us peace was on him, and by his wounds we are healed. We all, like sheep, have gone astray, each of us has turned to our own way; and the Lord has laid on him the iniquity of us all.** (Isaiah 53:5-6)

> **You see, at just the right time, when we were still powerless, Christ died for the ungodly. Very rarely will anyone die for a righteous person, though for**

a good person someone might possibly dare to die. But God demonstrates his own love for us in this: While we were still sinners, Christ died for us. (Romans 5:6-8)

Paid in Full

So we see that on the cross Jesus was suffering and dying on our behalf. He was receiving God's wrath and punishment for all the sins we have committed or would ever commit. He treated Jesus as if He were the one who committed all of our sins. The apostle Peter said of Jesus: **"'He himself bore our sins' in his body on the cross"** (1 Peter 2:24). When God's justice against all our sins was complete and the punishment for sin was totally paid for, Jesus, hanging on the cross, spoke these words: **"It is finished"** (John 19:30). The Greek word Jesus spoke here is *tetelastai*, which literally means, "paid in full." Jesus was saying that the punishment for sin was now complete and fully paid for by His suffering and sacrificial death on the cross.

Dead and Buried

After the penalty for sin was paid, the Bible says that Jesus bowed His head, gave up His spirit, and died. He was then taken off the cross by two men, Joseph of Arimathea and Nicodemus. The Bible records: **"Taking Jesus' body, the two of them wrapped it, with the spices, in strips of linen. This was in accordance with Jewish burial customs. At the place where Jesus was crucified, there was a garden, and in the garden a new tomb, in which no one had ever been laid. Because it was the Jewish day of Preparation and since the tomb was nearby, they laid Jesus there"** (John 19:40-42).

Risen and Ascended

The good news is, according to the Bible, three days later, Jesus came back to life, defeating death. The Bible says: **"After his** suffering, he presented himself to them and gave many convincing proofs that he was alive. He appeared to them over a period of forty days and spoke about the kingdom of God" (Acts 1:3). After these forty days, the Bible says that Jesus ascended back into heaven. The Gospel of Luke says: **"When he had led them out to the vicinity of Bethany, he lifted up his hands and blessed them. While he was blessing them, he left them and was taken up into heaven"** (Luke 24:50-51). The book of Acts describes the event this way, **"After he said this, he was taken up before their very eyes, and a cloud hid him from their sight. They were looking intently up into the sky as he was going, when suddenly two men dressed in white stood beside them. 'Men of Galilee,' they said, 'why do you stand here looking into the sky? This same Jesus, who has been taken from you into heaven, will come back in the same way you have seen him go into heaven'"** (Acts 1:9-11). Today, at this moment, the Bible says that Jesus is seated in heaven at the right hand of God the Father, waiting for the time when He will return to earth again.

Case Dismissed

This is the wonderful story of God's amazing love for us. It's called the Gospel, which literally means "good news". God, in His great love and mercy, made a way for us to be forgiven of our sins and to be made right with Him, so that we would be able to spend eternity in heaven with Him. God can now legally dismiss our case on Judgment Day. We can walk out of God's courtroom free and forgiven because Jesus stepped in and paid our fine in full.

The big question now is, what do I have to do to apply the payment Jesus made for me to my record? How do I receive the forgiveness God offers me through the suffering and death of Jesus Christ? Does it just automatically get applied to everyone? Does God just forgive everyone now and let them into heaven? As we learned previously, the answer is no, and only those who do *the will of the Father* that Jesus spoke of will have this payment applied to their record. Only they will be forgiven and only they will make it into the kingdom of heaven.

The Will of the Father

So finally we get to *the will of the Father.* What is *the will of the Father* that we must do to enter the kingdom of heaven? I am so excited to tell you. It has been very hard to put off telling you for so long, but it was necessary to talk about all that we did in order for you to truly understand how to make it to heaven.

The will of the Father that we must do to enter the kingdom of heaven is found throughout the New Testament part of the Bible, but a good place to start is with John 6:40, in which Jesus spells it out clearly: **"For *my Father's will* is that everyone who *looks to the Son* and *believes in him* shall have eternal life, and I will raise them up at the last day."** So *the will of the Father* is to *look to the Son and believe in Him*. This is what we must do to enter the kingdom of heaven.

Definition of Believe

Many at this point might say, "Well, I believe in Jesus, so I'm good to go." If you remember, *many* people who believe in Jesus and call Him Lord will be turned away from entering the kingdom of heaven. There will be many people in hell who merely *believed* in Jesus—even believed He died on the cross for their sins. Why? It has to do with our understanding of the word, *believe*. The word *believe* that Jesus used in John 6:40 doesn't mean to intellectually believe He existed or to mentally acknowledge the fact that He died on the cross for our sins. The word *"believe"* here means, *"to rely on"* or *"to trust in."* What Jesus is saying here is that only those who *look to Him* and *rely on what He did on the cross for them* will be forgiven of their sins and make it into heaven. To truly understand and grasp where you personally stand with this right now, go back again to your answer to this question: *"Why do you think Jesus should let you into heaven?"*

What Are You Relying On?

Look back again to your answer to this question, wherever you wrote it down. If you didn't write it down, try to remember what your answer was or simply answer the question again right now: *"Why do you think Jesus should let you into heaven?"* Remember, your answer to this question reveals what you are *relying on* to enter the kingdom of heaven. So what was your answer? What are you *relying on* to enter heaven?

Earlier, I gave my original answer to this question: "I believe in God, I try to go to church every Sunday, and I try to be a good person." Notice the common denominator in my answers is the word, "I." I was relying on or looking to myself, my religious works, and my own goodness to enter heaven. At that point in my life, if I would have died, it would have been with all my sins still on my record, and I would have had to pay the full penalty of my sins in hell for all eternity. Why? Because I had only intellectually believed in the existence of Jesus and mentally acknowledged the fact that He died for my sins. I wasn't looking to Him or relying on Him and what He did on the cross for me. I was relying on and looking to myself and what I could do.

That is exactly why the many people we looked at in the beginning missed entering heaven. They "believed" in Jesus intellectually, but they were still relying on what they could do themselves to enter heaven. Again, this is revealed in their words to Jesus: **"Lord, Lord, did we not prophesy in your name and in your name drive out demons and in your name perform many miracles?"** (Matthew 7:22). This is what they were relying on to enter the kingdom of heaven. They were not looking to Jesus, but to themselves. For that reason, their sins were not forgiven, they were still seen as "evildoers," and so they could not enter the kingdom of heaven.

Wrong Answer

Any who looks to themselves and relies on their own goodness, good deeds or religious works will not have their sins forgiven and will not enter the kingdom of heaven. If your answer to the question above involves any of the following, you will not make it into heaven:

- because I believe in God
- because I go to church
- because I was baptized
- because I confess my sins
- because I try my best to be a good person
- because I do a lot of good things; at least more good than bad
- because I pray, read the Bible, and give money to the church

Why won't those who rely on these things enter the kingdom of heaven? Notice again that the common denominator is the word, "I." They are not trusting in what Jesus has done for them to enter heaven. They are trusting in themselves, in what they can do, and how good they can be. If we could enter heaven by our own goodness, good deeds, or religious works then Jesus would not have had to come and die for our sins. These things will not get anyone into heaven.

"If we could enter heaven by our own goodness, good deeds, or religious works then Jesus would not have had to come and die for our sins."

Only those who do *the will of the Father* revealed in John 6:40 will have their sins forgiven and make it into heaven. The Father's will is that you *"look to the Son,"* not to yourself, and that you *"believe in Him,"* which again, means to rely on Him and what He did on the cross for you. You must not rely on trying to be a good person, doing good things, or any religious works. Here are some other scriptures that confirm what I am saying to you. As you read these verses and see the word, *believe,* remember that it means, "*to rely on*" or "*to trust in.*" It is not a mere intellectual belief in the existence of Jesus.

Confirming Verses

"For God so loved the world that he gave his one and only Son, that whoever *believes* in him shall not perish but have eternal life. For God did not send his Son into the world to condemn the world, but to save the world through him. Whoever *believes* in him is not condemned, but whoever does not believe stands condemned already because they have not believed in the name of God's one and only Son" (John 3:16-18).

This is saying that God loves you so much, He was willing to give His one and only Son to die for your sins. If you rely on what He did for you, you will not be condemned or perish in hell, but will have eternal life in heaven. It also says that those who aren't relying on Him stand condemned already.

"Whoever *believes* in the Son has eternal life, but whoever rejects the Son will not see life, for God's wrath remains on them" (John 3:36).

Again, we see that only those who believe in the Son, who are relying on Him, receive eternal life. Those who reject the Son will not receive eternal life. God's wrath, His condemnation, is still the sentence hanging over those who reject the Son, because their sins have not been forgiven. People can reject the Son of God in two different ways. First, they can deny Him outright. The other way is a little more subtle. People who are relying on their own goodness, good deeds, or religious works to enter heaven are in fact rejecting the Son and the provision God has made. They are seeking to enter heaven by their own way, not God's. What they are really saying is, "Jesus, I really don't need you or your sacrifice on the cross, because I can get into heaven my own way."

"Then they asked him, 'What must we do to do the works God requires?' Jesus answered, 'The work of God is this: to *believe* in the one he has sent'" (John 6:28-29).

These people wanted to know what kind of "works" God requires to have His approval and acceptance. Jesus revealed that the only work God requires is to *believe* or rely on the one God sent to earth, Jesus Christ.

"For it is by grace you have been saved, through faith— and this is not from yourselves, it is the gift of God—not by works, so that no one can boast" (Ephesians 2:8-9).

This verse is very powerful and makes things so very clear that it is worth taking a moment to break it down to truly understand it.

"For it is by *grace* you have been saved" (Ephesians 2:8)

This means we are saved from our sins and the hell we deserve only by God's grace. This means that it cannot be earned or deserved by anything we could ever do or how good we can be.

"through *faith*" (Ephesians 2:8)

Only through faith can we receive this offer of forgiveness. Faith carries the same meaning as the word, believe, which is, "to rely on" or "trust in."

"and this is not from yourselves, it is the *gift* of God" (Ephesians 2:8)

Salvation from sin is a free *gift* from God. A gift is not something you earn or deserve. It is something given because of the love of the one giving it. If someone wanted to give you a brand new car as a free gift and you said, "Hey, at least let me give you $100 for it," they would probably be insulted by that, and it would no longer be a gift. God saving us from our sins and giving us eternal life in heaven is a free gift, and if we try to somehow earn it or pay for it even a little bit, it no longer remains a gift and is an insult to God. The fact that eternal life is a gift and cannot be earned is confirmed in Romans 6:23, **"For the wages of sin is death, but the *gift* of God is eternal life in Christ Jesus our Lord."** This means that what we have earned (wages) and deserve because of our sin is death, which in this context means eternal separation from God in hell. Thankfully we don't have to receive what we actually deserve. God offers us eternal life as a free gift, and it is only found in Jesus Christ and received only by those who put their trust in Him.

"not by works, so that no one can boast"** (Ephesians 2:9)

Being saved from our sins and receiving eternal life in heaven is not obtained by our good works, so no one can boast, saying: "I went to church," "I gave to the poor," "I was baptized," or "I was a good person." This type of boasting reminds me of the group of many people who boasted to Jesus: **"Lord, Lord, did we not prophesy in your name and in your name drive out demons and in your name perform many miracles?"** (Matthew 7:22). On Judgment Day many will boast about all their good works, but will not enter heaven because they didn't know or understand that it cannot be obtained by their good works, but only by faith in Jesus.

Notice that all the verses quoted above make no mention of having to be baptized, going to church, confessing our sins, being good enough, or doing enough good deeds. Notice also that they do not say to rely on Jesus *plus* your own goodness, or Jesus *plus* your good deeds, or Jesus *plus* your religious works. The sacrifice of Jesus on the cross was sufficient to pay for all your sins and make you right with God. When Jesus said, **"It is finished"** (John 19:30), He meant that it was finished and there is nothing you can do to add to what He did on the cross. He calls you to simply believe and rely on what He did for you.

A Living Illustration

To make it abundantly clear that eternal life in heaven is received only through faith in Jesus and not by our own goodness or good deeds, God Himself provided a living illustration in His Word. The Bible says that two criminals were also crucified with Jesus, one on his left and one on his right. At the beginning of their crucifixion, both of these criminals mocked and insulted Jesus. The Bible says, **"Those crucified with him also heaped insults on him"** (Mark 15:32). However, we see that at one point during those hours he spent on the cross next to Jesus, one of the criminals had a change of heart. Here is the Bible account: **"One of the criminals who hung there hurled insults at him: 'Aren't you the Messiah? Save yourself and us!' But the other criminal rebuked him. 'Don't you fear God,' he said, 'since you are under the same sentence? We are punished justly, for we are getting what our deeds deserve. But this man has done nothing wrong.' Then he said, 'Jesus, remember me when you come into your kingdom.' Jesus answered him, 'Truly I tell you, today you will be with me in paradise'"** (Luke 23:39-43). This one criminal started out his crucifixion going along with those around him, hurling insults at Jesus. But somewhere along the way something changed. The man went from insulting Jesus to defending Him and putting his faith in Him.

Like many people who are on their deathbed, this man probably began to think about where he would spend eternity, which can be frightening if you don't know for sure you are going to heaven. This man, being a criminal, may have realized he probably wasn't sitting so good with God at the moment, and was on his way to hell. Perhaps this was due to something Jesus said during those long hours on the cross. We don't know. Somehow, somewhere along the way, this man realized that the man dying next to him was the King of heaven, for he said, **"Jesus, remember me when you come into *your kingdom*"** (Luke 23:42). Somehow this man realized Jesus was dying for his sins, so he put his faith in the only one who could save him from the hell he deserved. This man was a criminal and nailed to a cross. He couldn't get baptized. He couldn't do any good deeds. He couldn't do anything! However, he could do the one thing God requires of us to enter His kingdom; he put his trust in the death of Jesus Christ as the payment for his sins. And Jesus said to him, **"Truly I tell you, today you will be with me in paradise"** (Luke 23:43). This man was moments away from his death and moments away from spending eternity in hell. He just made it into heaven, not because he was good, and not because he did any good deeds or religious works, but because he did *the will of the Father* in heaven: *He looked to the Son and believed in Him.*

Jesus Is the Only Way

Jesus Christ and His death on the cross is your only hope of making it to heaven. In fact, *He is the only way into heaven.* Before Jesus was crucified, He told His followers that He would soon be leaving them and going back to the Father in heaven. He said to them, **"You know *the way* to the place where I am going"** (John 14:4). One of His followers, Thomas, replied, **"Lord, we don't know where you are going, so how can we know *the way*?"** (John 14:5). **"Jesus answered, '*I am the way* and the truth and the life. *No one comes to the Father except through me*'"** (John 14:6). Jesus told His followers that He was the way to heaven and that no one could get there to be with the Father except through

Him. The Bible confirms this in Acts 4:12: **"Salvation is found in no one else, for there is no other name under heaven given to mankind by which we must be saved."**

"Jesus Christ and His death on the cross is your only hope of making it to heaven. In fact, *He is the only way into heaven.*"

This statement of exclusivity makes many people angry at Christians, but Christians are not the ones who started it; Jesus did. If we were to say there is some other way to heaven, or that all religions are equal and lead to God, we would be lying and calling Jesus a liar. So what about Muslims, Buddhists, Hindus, Jews, and all the other religions out there. Are they all wrong? According to the words of Jesus above, yes. Jesus Christ is the only one who died for your sins and the sins of the entire world. No other person or religion has made provision for the forgiveness of sins. Also, of all the religious leaders in history, Jesus is the only one who was both fully man and fully God. Jesus is the only one who did amazing miracles. He is the only one who was raised from the dead. All other religious leaders who have died are still dead and in their graves, but the grave of Jesus is empty! He is risen and alive!

Jesus said in John 10:9, **"I am the gate; whoever enters through me will be saved."** Jesus Christ is the only way into the kingdom of heaven. He is the gate and only those who enter through Him, by relying on His sacrifice, will enter. Remember what Jesus said in Matthew 7:13-14: **"Enter through the narrow gate. For wide is the gate and broad is the road that leads to destruction, and many enter through it. But small is the gate and narrow the road that leads to life, and only a few find it."** Jesus is the "narrow gate" that leads into the kingdom of heaven. It's narrow because He is the only way in. The gate is wide and the road is broad that leads to destruction because the majority of people think that the way into heaven is through trying to be a good person, doing good things, some religious works, or some other religion.

Offered to All

The Bible says, **"For there is one God and one mediator between God and mankind, the man Christ Jesus, who gave himself as a ransom for *all* people"** (1 Timothy 2:5-6). It says here that Jesus gave Himself as a ransom or payment for *all* mankind. *This is not exclusive at all!* Jesus died for Muslims, Buddhists, Hindus, Jews, and the entire world. Remember John 3:16: **"For God so loved the world that he gave his one and only Son, that whoever believes in him shall not perish but have eternal life."** God's love and His offer of forgiveness and eternal life through His Son is not exclusive, it is for the entire world, and is received by *whoever* believes. This offer is for everyone!

"God's love and His offer of forgiveness and eternal life through His Son is not exclusive, it is for the entire world, and is received by *whoever* believes."

What Should You Do?

So what should you do? First of all, you need examine where your trust has been. What have you been relying on to enter the kingdom of heaven? If it has anything to do with trying to be good enough, the good things you have done, or any religious works, like baptism or going to church, you must stop trusting in these things immediately. These things will not get you into heaven. Next you need to simply transfer that trust, from yourself (and what you can do) to Jesus and what He did for you on the cross. The Bible makes it clear over and over again that it is by our faith in Jesus Christ alone that we receive forgiveness for our sins and eternal life in heaven.

To express your faith in Jesus Christ and to receive God's offer of forgiveness and the free gift of eternal life, you could pray a prayer something like the one below. The words are not important. It's not a magical prayer that saves you. Again, it is your faith in Jesus that saves you. That faith can be expressed through this prayer:

> *Jesus, I realize that I have sinned against you many times and in many ways. I have broken your Laws, and I know that I deserve to be in hell. But I thank you that you loved me enough to come and pay my fine by taking my punishment on the cross. Thank you for dying for me. This moment, I no longer rely on my own goodness, good deeds, or religious works to enter heaven. I rely on you alone and what you did for me on the cross. Jesus, I call on you today to save me from my sins and the hell I deserve. I put my hope and trust in you alone. And with your help, I will turn from the things you show me are wrong or sinful. Jesus, I ask these things in your name. Amen.*

You Have Made a Decision

It is my hope and prayer that you have made the decision to trust Jesus as your Savior. There is no other decision more important than this one. But you need to know that to *not* make this decision right now, *is to make a decision*. It's a decision not to believe the Word of God and a decision to reject Jesus, His sacrifice on the cross, His offer of forgiveness and your place in heaven. To not make this decision this very moment is to risk the possibility of spending eternity in hell, because you may not have another minute to live. God wants to save you from your sins and the punishment you deserve, but you must personally make the decision to put your faith in Jesus. No one can do it for you. Please don't play with your eternal destiny. Make this decision today, before it's too late. If you die before making this decision, it will be too late. It will mean hell for all eternity, with no hope or chance of ever getting out. That's how serious this decision is and how important it is that you make this decision right now!

If you have chosen to put your faith in Jesus and His death on the cross, and have genuinely called on Him to save you from your sins, you can be assured that He has heard you. He has forgiven you and He has saved you because He is faithful to keep His promises.

When you trust Jesus as your Savior, not only do you receive forgiveness for your sins and eternal life in heaven, but you receive many other blessings as well. Here is a list of just a few of the many wonderful things that happen to you when you trust Jesus Christ as your Savior:

1. You are made alive spiritually and reborn (born again).

    - **"In his great mercy he has given us new birth into a living hope through the resurrection of Jesus Christ from the dead"** (1 Peter 1:3).

2. You become a child of God.

    - **"Yet to all who did receive him, to those who believed in his name, he gave the right to become children of God"** (John 1:12).

3. God the Holy Spirit comes to live inside of you.

    - **"Do you not know that your bodies are temples of the Holy Spirit, who is in you, whom you have received from God?"** (1 Corinthians 6:19).

4. You are reconciled with God and become holy in His sight.

    - **"Once you were alienated from God and were enemies in your minds because of your evil behavior. But now he has reconciled you by Christ's physical body through death to present you holy in his sight, without blemish and free from accusation"** (Colossians 1:21-22).

5. You are made perfect in God's eyes.

   • **"For by one sacrifice he has made perfect forever those who are being made holy"** (Hebrews 10:14).

6. You are now at peace with God.

   • **"Therefore, since we have been justified through faith, we have peace with God through our Lord Jesus Christ"** (Romans 5:1).

This is just a very small list of things that happen to you once you turn to Jesus and put your faith in Him. I encourage you to read through the Bible yourself and discover all the amazing things God does for you once you accept the sacrifice of His Son on your behalf.

Chapter 5

RESPONDING WITH REPENTANCE

Although we are saved from our sins and make it into heaven by God's grace, through faith in Jesus Christ alone, God still calls us to repent or turn from sin. Repentance is not something we do to earn our place in heaven, but it is a response to what God has done for us.

To understand that repentance does not save us from our sins, let's recall the illustration we looked at in chapter three. A man guilty of rape and murder stands before a judge pleading: "Judge, yes, I raped and murdered those women, but I have turned from my ways and I will never do these things again. Please let me go." Is the judge going to let him go because he has turned from his evil ways and promises not to do it again? Of course not. In the same way, turning from our sins isn't going to wash them away or get us into heaven.

We are saved from our sins not because we stop doing bad things, but only because Jesus stepped in and paid our fine. It is our faith in Jesus and relying on what He did that allows that payment to be applied to our record.

To better understand the place that repentance plays in our faith, it might be helpful to know the true meaning of the word, *repent.* The New Testament part of the Bible was originally written in Greek, and the Greek word for repent is *metanoeo*, which literally means, "to change one's mind." In the context of Scripture, this word means "a change of mind that results in a change of action or behavior."

Do a U-turn

Repentance starts when we *change our minds* about Jesus by putting our faith in Him to save us instead of our own works or goodness. Repentance also includes *changing our minds* about sin, which results in turning away from sin with the help of God. This is not just an academic change of mind, but a radical turning away from sin. The picture of repentance is doing a 180 or U-turn. To receive God's forgiveness, we are turning toward Jesus and putting our faith in Him. In doing this, naturally we turn away from sin because God and sin are in opposite directions. You can't turn toward Jesus for forgiveness without moving away from a life of sin.

There are many different reasons why we should turn from sin. For most of this chapter we will explore four of those reasons.

Gratitude for the Cross

One of the reasons we should turn from sin is out of gratitude for what Jesus did for us on the cross. Repentance is a natural response after you see clearly what Jesus did on the cross for you. This response is revealed clearly in Titus 2:11-14: "**For the grace of God that brings salvation has appeared to all men. It teaches us to say 'No' to ungodliness and worldly passions, and to live self-controlled, upright and godly lives in this present age, while we wait for the blessed hope—the glorious appearing of our great God and Savior, Jesus Christ, who gave himself for us to redeem us from all wickedness and to purify for himself a people that are his very own, eager to do what is good**" (NIV1984). Jesus and His gruesome death on the cross is "***the grace of God that brings salvation***" (Titus 2:11, NIV1984). It is a clear picture of His suffering and death that "**teaches us to** say 'No' to ungodliness and worldly passions, and to live self-controlled, upright and godly lives" (Titus 2:12).

"Repentance is a natural response after you see clearly what Jesus did on the cross for you."

Jesus suffered intensely and was brutally killed because of our sins. Why would we want to go back to or continue doing what caused Him to suffer and die in the first place? Romans 2:4 says, **"Or do you show contempt for the riches of his kindness, forbearance and patience, not realizing that God's kindness is intended to lead you to repentance."** When we see God's kindness revealed in the cross of Jesus, it should cause us to turn away from sin out of gratitude for what He has done for us.

Love for God

Another closely related reason we should turn from sin is out of love for God in response to the great love He has shown us. The Bible says, **"We love because he first loved us"** (1 John 4:19). Our response to the love that God has shown us by sending Jesus to die for our sins is to love Him back.

So how does Scripture say we can show our love for God? Well, in 1 John 5:3 it says, **"This is love for God: *to obey his commands*"** (NIV1984). That's pretty straightforward and simple; we show our love for God by obeying His commands. And Jesus had this to say in the Gospel of John, **"Whoever has my commands and *obeys* them, he is the one who loves me"** (John 14:21, NIV1984). He says in John 14:23, **"If anyone loves me, he will *obey* my teaching"** (NIV1984). In John 14:24, He continues by saying, **"He who does not love me will *not obey* my teaching"** (NIV1984). We can see clearly from the scriptures above that the way we are called to show our love for Jesus is to obey His commands and teachings found in the Bible. When we don't obey His teachings we are actually revealing our lack of love for Him.

One of the commands that Jesus has given us is to *repent*. Matthew 4:17 says, **"From that time on Jesus began to preach, 'Repent, for the kingdom of heaven is near'"** (NIV1984). Jesus also had this to say, twice in one chapter, **"But unless you repent, you too will all perish"** (Luke 13:3, 5). So if we aren't changing our minds about sin and turning from it, not only does it reveal our lack of love for Jesus, but it may also reveal that our faith is not genuine and we haven't been truly saved from our sins. But if we have truly been saved and truly love Jesus, we will turn from our sins and obey His commands and teachings.

Future Judgment

Another important reason and motivation for repentance is the fact that we will all one day have to give an account for our lives and be judged for how we lived. If you have genuinely turned to Jesus and put your faith in Him, you will not be judged to determine *where* you will spend eternity; that was taken care of at the cross and by your faith in Jesus. You will, however, be judged on how you lived your life for Jesus. That will determine how you will be rewarded in heaven. How you live as a believer will still impact your life in Heaven for all eternity.

"How you live as a believer will still impact your life in Heaven for all eternity."

One of the famous lines from the movie, *Gladiator,* is so true, "What we do in life echoes in eternity." The apostle Paul said in 2 Corinthians 5:9-10, **"So we make it our goal to please him, whether we are at home in the body or away from it. For we must all appear before the judgment seat of Christ, so that each of us may receive what is due us for the things done while in the body, whether good or bad."** Because we as believers still have to stand before the judgment seat of Christ and give an account for how we lived, we should seek to live lives that are pleasing to Him in every way. This means that with His help we will seek to turn away from all sin.

Sin Is Destructive

Another reason we should turn from sin is the fact that it is always destructive and harmful. In the book of Galatians 6:7-8 it says, **"Do not be deceived: God cannot be mocked. A man reaps what he sows. The one who sows to please his sinful nature, from that nature will reap destruction; the one who sows to please the Spirit, from the Spirit will reap eternal life"** (NIV1984). If we try to satisfy our sinful desires by doing things that go against God's ways, we will bring destruction into our lives. God doesn't tell us to turn from sin to keep us from having fun, but to keep us safe and give us the best life possible. God is the one who created us. He knows what is best for us and He wants the best for us. He has given us commands and rules to live by to make that all possible. God said in Deuteronomy 5:29, **"Oh, that their hearts would be inclined to fear me and keep all my commands always,** *so that it might go well with them and their children forever!"* When we obey God's commands things will go well with us and our children. When we disobey, things don't go so well.

"God doesn't tell us to turn from sin to keep us from having fun, but to keep us safe and give us the best life possible."

Sin may be pleasurable for a time, but you will always reap its destructive consequences at some point. Drunkenness, premarital sex, adultery, pornography, stealing, lying, and all other sins will negatively affect your life in some way or another, to some degree or another. However, it won't just affect you, it will also have a negative effect on the lives of other people around you too. Sin destroys many marriages, ruins the lives of many children, and destroys many friendships. We should seek to turn away from all sin because it is never good for us or for those around us, even if we don't see the immediate consequences. In the end, sin is always destructive.

Help From the Holy Spirit

Right now it might seem impossible to turn away from some of the sins you are struggling with or have been enjoying. You may feel like you don't have the power or even the desire to turn away from these sins. It is important to remember that one of the amazing things that happens to you the moment you put your faith in Jesus to save you is that the Holy Spirit comes to live inside you. He gives you both the power and the desire to turn away from the sins in your life. If you have truly put your faith in Jesus, the Holy Spirit lives in you, and repentance is inevitable; it will happen.

When the Holy Spirit comes to live inside us, He gives us a new heart with new desires. He makes us into a new person from the inside out. The Bible says that we actually become new creations of God, totally new people on the inside. Second Corinthians 5:17 says, **"Therefore, if anyone is in Christ, he is a *new creation*; the old has gone, the new has come!"** (NIV1984).

My Story

After I put my faith in Jesus, my heart and life changed radically. I no longer wanted to get drunk, commit sexual immorality, or sin in any way against God. This was not only out of gratitude for what Jesus did for me on the cross, but also because the Holy Spirit came to live inside me and gave me a new heart with new desires. I wanted to do what was right in every way and live a life that was pleasing to God. I felt guilty about things that I had never before felt guilty about. I stopped going to bars and getting drunk with my friends. I broke off a relationship with a girl that involved sexual sin. My family and friends probably thought I was a little weird and may have wondered what had happened to me because I was a totally different person. I wasn't perfect and I wasn't sinless, but

I knew I was different. I knew I had a different relationship toward sin. I no longer ran after sin and embraced it, but tried to run from it and battled against it.

Justification vs. Sanctification

When you put your faith in Jesus and are *saved*, the Bible says that you are "*justified*" before God. This is a legal term that means God has declared you "*not guilty*" and "*innocent*" before Him. Using a play on words, it's now "just-if-ied" never sinned. All my sins are forgiven; past, present, and future. I now look perfect before God.

When you get saved, the Holy Spirit comes to live in you and He begins the process of what the Bible calls "*sanctification*," which means, "*to be made holy*." The Holy Spirit begins the process of making us more and more like Jesus. The Scripture says that we **"are being transformed into his likeness with ever-increasing glory, which comes from the Lord, who is the Spirit"** (2 Corinthians 3:18, NIV1984). Notice where it says this transformation comes from—the Spirit—not from our own striving and struggling or anything of ourselves. So when we defeat a sin in our lives or see our character improving, we can't be prideful or take credit for it. The praise and glory goes to the Holy Spirit, who is working in our lives and changing us. But we do have a part to play. We are called to work with the Holy Spirit and yield to Him as He works in us and seeks to change us and make us more like Jesus.

The Bible says we can actually resist the Holy Spirit and grieve Him. This happens when we disobey Him or continue in something He is trying to remove from our lives. This process of sanctification is a partnership with the Holy Spirit. He is the only one who can make us more like Jesus, but it won't go so well if we are working against Him. The more obedient and yielded to the Holy Spirit we are the easier and quicker this transformation process will go.

This process of *sanctification* is a lifelong process; it doesn't happen overnight. There are some sins and character flaws that will go away immediately. Others are stronger and deeper and will try to hang on. These may take years to get rid of, but the Holy Spirit is faithful and He will not give up on you. The Bible says that, **"he who began a good work in you will carry it on to completion until the day of Christ Jesus"** (Philippians 1:6). This means God is going to be working in your life to make you more and more like Jesus until the day Jesus returns to earth or until you die— whichever comes first.

Live Holy

Just below, I quote a few Scriptures that reveal God's call to believers to live lives that are holy and pleasing to Him. This lifestyle is not to earn our way into heaven but it is our response to His love for us. With His help and power, this is how we should seek to live:

> **But among you there must not be even a hint of sexual immorality, or any kind of impurity, or of greed, because these are improper for God's holy people. Nor should there be obscenity, foolish talk or coarse joking, which are out of place, but rather thanksgiving.** (Ephesians 5:3-4)

> **Put to death, therefore, whatever belongs to your earthly nature: sexual immorality, impurity, lust, evil desires and greed, which is idolatry. Because of these, the wrath of God is coming. You used to walk in these ways, in the life you once lived. But now you must also rid yourselves of all such things as these: anger, rage, malice, slander, and filthy language from your lips. Do not lie to each other, since you have taken off your old self with its practices and have put on the new self, which is being renewed in knowledge in the image of its Creator.** (Colossians 3:5-10)

It is God's will that you should be sanctified: that you should avoid sexual immorality; that each of you should learn to control your own body in a way that is holy and honorable, not in passionate lust like the pagans, who do not know God; and that in this matter no one should wrong or take advantage of a brother or sister. The Lord will punish all those who commit such sins, as we told you and warned you before. For God did not call us to be impure, but to live a holy life. Therefore, anyone who rejects this instruction does not reject a human being but God, the very God who gives you his Holy Spirit. (1 Thessalonians 4:3-8)

As obedient children, do not conform to the evil desires you had when you lived in ignorance. But just as he who called you is holy, so be holy in all you do; for it is written: 'Be holy, because I am holy.' (1 Peter 1:14-16)

Chapter 6

HOW CAN I BE CERTAIN?

At this point you may say to me: "Okay, I believe everything you have told me so far, but how can I really be 100 percent certain that I will make it to heaven when I die? How can I be sure that I have been *born again?*" The Bible tells us there is certain evidence that should be in the life of a genuine believer, some outward and inward signs that he or she is truly born again. In His day apostle Paul challenged those who professed to be believers by saying, **"Examine yourselves to see whether you are in the faith; test yourselves. Do you not realize that Christ Jesus is in you—unless, of course, you fail the test?"** (2 Corinthians 13:5). Paul is saying that you should examine yourself and your life to see if your faith is genuine and if there is any evidence that Jesus Christ is in your life. If there is no evidence that Jesus is in your life, then you have failed the test and your faith is not genuine—you are not saved and will not make it into heaven.

Preliminary Questions

Before getting into the specific evidence of a true believer, here are some preliminary questions to ask yourself first:

- Do you realize you have sinned against God by breaking His Laws? Do you understand that because of this, you are not good by God's standard, but are seen as a guilty criminal deserving punishment in hell?

- Do you understand that no amount of good works, holy living, or any religious works can ever take away your sin or make up for them? Do you understand there is nothing you can do on your own to make yourself acceptable to God or get you into heaven?

- Have you done *the will of the Father* that will alone get you into heaven? In other words, are you looking to Jesus and relying on His sacrifice alone to take away your sins and make you right with God?

- Out of love for Jesus and gratefulness for all He has done for you, and with the help of the Holy Spirit, are you ready and willing to turn away from all sin in your life?

If you can genuinely and sincerely say "yes" to the things listed above, you can have confidence that you are saved and will make it to heaven when you die.

Don't Rely on Being Perfect

There are a couple other things you can do to gain the assurance that you will make it to heaven. First, you must *not* rely on living a perfect, sinless life. Remember, you don't get into heaven because you are living a perfect and sin-free life, but only because of your faith in what Jesus did for you on the cross. Even those who are born again face temptations and even stumble into sin. However, they do not lose their right standing with God or their place in heaven every time they sin. If that were the case, no one would make it into heaven.

Don't Rely on Feelings

To gain the assurance that you are going to heaven you must also *not* rely on your feelings. There are so many things that affect our emotions, driving them up and down and all over the place every day, so we can't rely on them to *feel* whether or not we are saved. One day might be great, spiritually speaking. You walk in holiness and obedience to the Lord and really *feel* like you are saved. The next day might not be so great. You fight against some temptation or stumble into some sin and now you don't *feel* like you are saved at all. Our feelings don't determine whether or not we have been saved. Our faith in Jesus saves us, and faith is not a feeling.

**"Our feelings don't determine whether or not
we have been saved. Our faith in Jesus saves us,
and faith is not a feeling."**

Rely on the Cross

To gain the assurance that you have been saved and are going to heaven, you must have something solid and unchanging to stand upon, something that is outside of yourself and doesn't depend on you. So the first thing you must rely on is the historical and unchanging fact of the sacrifice of Jesus on the cross for your sins. It's a done deal! Nothing can take away or change what Jesus did for you. He died on the cross so you could be forgiven and enter heaven.

Rely on God's Promises

The next thing you must rely on if you want to have the assurance that you are going to heaven is the solid and unchanging promises found in God's Word. Because of who God is, He cannot lie and cannot go back on His promises. Jesus gave us a promise in John 3:16: **"For God so loved the world that he gave his one and only Son, that whoever believes in him shall not perish but have eternal life."** He gave us another promise in John 3:36: **"Whoever believes in the Son has eternal life, but whoever rejects the Son will not see life, for God's wrath remains on them."** Jesus gives us still another promise in John 6:40: **"For my Father's will** is that everyone who looks to the Son and believes in him shall have eternal life, and I will raise them up at the last day." If you have genuinely put your faith in Jesus, you can claim these promises, stand upon them, and find peace and rest in them. God is faithful and He will keep His promises. You can trust Him to do what He has promised to do. If you ever want to be 100 percent certain that you have been saved and will make it to heaven, you have to learn to rely on these two unchanging things: the sacrifice Jesus made on the cross for you and the related promises found in God's Word.

Self-Examination

If you want to be certain that you have been genuinely saved and will make it to heaven when you die, you must also examine your life for evidence that something has happened to you, that you are different. Although we don't rely on living a perfect life, if we have been truly saved, our hearts and lives will be different. If you have been genuinely saved there should be some evidence of this in your life. As the apostle Paul said, we must examine and test ourselves to see if there is any evidence that Jesus Christ is in our lives.

"Although we don't rely on living a perfect life, if we have been truly saved, our hearts and lives will be different."

In the Bible we find specific evidence that should be in the life of anyone who has genuinely put his or her faith in Jesus and is truly born again. The Bible book 1 John was actually written for this very purpose. In the time the apostle John lived, just as today, many people claimed to be followers of Jesus, but some were genuine and some were false. John wanted to help believers know the genuine from the false, so he wrote about specific evidence that should be in any true believer's life. If someone did not have these things in his or her life, believers would know he or she was not a genuine believer. These are not things that make us right with God or get us into heaven, they are the results, or proof of genuine faith. They are evidence that someone has truly been born again and saved from their sins. Let's now take a look at four of those evidences and see how we measure up.

Obedience to God

One of the evidences that should be in the life of a genuine believer is revealed in 1 John 2:3-6: **"We know that we have come to know him *if we keep his commands*. Whoever says, 'I know him,' but does not do what he commands is a liar, and the truth is not in that person. But if anyone *obeys his word*, love for God is truly made complete in them. This is how we know we are in him: Whoever claims to live in him must live as Jesus did."** John says here that one of the ways we can tell we are genuine believers and truly know God is whether or not we obey His commands. As mentioned earlier, when someone puts their faith in Jesus Christ to save them from their sins, the Holy Spirit comes to live inside of them and He will give them both the desire and power to obey God's commands. Someone who has not been genuinely saved does not have the Holy Spirit living in them, so they will not have the desire or power to obey God's commands.

A life marked by obedience to God and His Word is proof that our faith is genuine and we have been born again. This does not mean we will live perfect lives but that the normal pattern of our lives will change from one of disobedience to obedience. This also means that someone who has been genuinely saved will now have a desire to read God's Word, which contains His commands. How can we obey His commands if we don't know what they are? If someone has no desire to read God's Word or know His commands and obey them, this is evidence they are not a genuine believer and have not been born again.

Before I put my faith in Jesus Christ and was born again, I had little or no concern about knowing and obeying God's commands. I also had no desire to read the Bible. However, after I put my faith in Jesus and was born again, I had a great hunger and thirst to read God's Word and to know and obey His commands. It's been over twenty years since I made my decision for Jesus, and this hunger and thirst is still alive in me today. Over the years, I have been growing in obedience to God's Word. I haven't reached perfection yet, but there has definitely been progress. This is evidence that my faith is genuine, that I have truly been saved, and it gives me assurance that I will make it to heaven. My obedience to God's Word doesn't earn my place in heaven; it's proof that I have been born again and genuinely saved from my sins.

Though genuine believers may not be perfectly obedient all the time, especially when they first get saved, as they grow and mature as believers, they should grow in obedience. If you are genuinely saved your life will be changing and growing from disobedience to obedience. This is evidence that your faith is genuine, that you have been born again and gives you the assurance that you will make it to heaven.

"If you are genuinely saved your life will be changing and growing from disobedience to obedience."

Decreasing Sin

John gives a related area of evidence for a genuine believer in 1 John 3:6-10:

> No one who lives in him *keeps on sinning.* No one who *continues to sin* has either seen him or known him. Dear children, do not let anyone lead you astray. The one who does what is right is righteous, just as he is righteous. The one who does what is sinful is of the devil, because the devil has been sinning from the beginning. The reason the Son of God appeared was to destroy the devil's work. No one who is born of God will *continue to sin*, because God's seed remains in him; they cannot *go on sinning*, because they have been born of God. This is

how we know who the children of God are and who the children of the devil are: Anyone who does not do what is right is not God's child.

Wow! This sounds like a tough one, if not an impossible one. But before you get frustrated or discouraged, you need to know that John is not saying here that a genuine believer never sins but that he doesn't "*keep on sinning*," meaning his lifestyle is not one marked by habitual, continuous sin that goes unchecked. Though at times a genuine believer will still struggle with sin and may even at times get stuck in a sin that is hard to get out of, they won't want to stay in it and will do all they can to get it out of their life. A genuine believer will also not be able to enjoy sin as they once did before they were saved. They will now feel bad about their sin.

I have known some men, genuine believers, who have struggled with pornography. Some even developed an addiction to it. Yet the reason I knew they were genuine believers was because when they gave in to it, they felt horrible about it, they hated it, confessed it, and did everything they could to keep it out of their lives. Someone who is not genuinely saved will not hate sin, but love it. They will not confess their sin, but try to hide it. They will not try to fight against sin, but will embrace it without any guilt or shame. In the passage above John is saying that those who willfully keep on sinning without any problem with it are not genuine believers; they don't really know God.

Before I put my faith in Jesus and was saved, I had no concern about getting sin out of my life, but rather enjoyed it. I enjoyed lust, pornography, and sexual immorality. I enjoyed getting drunk, cursing, and many other sins. However, as I mentioned in the previous chapter, after I got saved, my heart and life radically changed. I now felt guilty about these things and had a desire to turn away from them and do what was right and pleasing to God. I could no longer enjoy these things as I once did. It's not that I no longer sinned and began living a perfect life, but my attitude and relationship to sin had radically changed. I no longer ran after and embraced sin, but tried to run away from it and get it out of my life. Sin began to decrease in my life. This was not something I could have done on my own, and not something I even had a desire to do before I was saved. This was evidence that something had happened to me, that I had been genuinely born again. This helped give me the assurance that my faith was genuine and that I would make it to heaven.

In the passage above John says, **"No one who is born of God will continue to sin, because God's seed remains in them; they cannot go on sinning, because they have been born of God"** (1John 3:9). John says here that the reason a genuine believer won't continue to sin is because they have been "born of God," and "God's seed," meaning the Holy Spirit, lives inside of them. Once again, when someone trusts Jesus as their Savior, the Holy Spirit comes to live inside them and He gives them new desires and the power to do what is right. Remember, it's not that the genuine believer won't ever sin, it means sin won't be the habitual practice of his or her life. John ends this passage of Scripture by revealing that only two kinds of children exist in the world today: children of God and children of Satan. No one can belong to both families at the same time. Either one belongs to God's family and displays God's righteous character or one belongs to Satan's family and displays his sinful nature. So if your life is one that could be described as growing in holiness, and sin is decreasing in your life, then you can have assurance that you are genuinely saved and will make it to heaven.

"Either one belongs to God's family and displays God's righteous character or one belongs to Satan's family and displays his sinful nature."

Love for Believers

John gives another mark of a genuine believer in 1 John 3:14-15: **"We know that we have passed from death to life, *because we love each other*. Anyone who does not love remains in**

death. Anyone who hates a brother or sister is a murderer, and you know that no murderer has eternal life residing in him." John is saying here that we can have assurance that we have gone from being spiritually dead to being spiritually alive (born again), because we love our brothers and sisters in the family of God. This means that anyone who does not have a genuine love for the family of God is still spiritually dead and separated from God. A genuine believer will have a desire to be around other believers. This would include having a desire to go to church. This is not just so they can say they went to church or to make them feel better, but because they have or want to have genuine, loving relationships with those in the family of God. Someone who is not a genuine believer will have little or no desire to go to church or be around other believers.

Before I put my faith in Jesus and was born again, I didn't have much desire to go to church. Most of the time I actually dreaded the thought of going. When I did have the desire to go, it was for the wrong reason. I thought if I went to church, it would make God happy with me and better my chances of getting into heaven. It also helped take away the guilt of sin and made me feel better about myself, especially after a weekend of drunkenness and sexual immorality. As we learned in the previous chapters, going to church has nothing to do with helping us get into heaven. Our motive for attending church shouldn't be to make us feel better about ourselves. We should have a desire to go to church because we love God and other believers, and because we have a desire to learn more about God and His Word.

After I got saved, I couldn't wait to go to church on Sunday. It was the highlight of my week. I no longer went to try and earn God's favor and my place in heaven, or to take away my guilt and make me feel better about myself. Because of my faith in what Jesus did for me on the cross, I already had all these things and more. I now had God's favor and a secure place in heaven. I didn't have to try and earn these things by going to church. I now went to church because I wanted to worship God, hear some good teaching from the Word of God, and because I had a genuine love for other believers. This was all evidence that I had truly been born again, and it helped give me assurance that I was saved and would make it to heaven.

Jesus said that the number one trademark of a genuine believer is love for other believers. In John 13:34-35, Jesus says, **"A new command I give you: Love one another. As I have loved you, so you must love one another. *By this* everyone will know that you are my disciples, *if you love one another.*"** This is not talking about any type of romantic love, the normal love between a husband and wife, or the love of a parent for his or her children. This is talking about a supernatural and sacrificial love that comes only from God.

In 1 John 3:16-18, John describes what this type of love looks like: **"This is how we know what love is: Jesus Christ laid down his life for us. And we ought to lay down our lives for our brothers and sisters. If anyone has material possessions and sees a brother or sister in need but has no pity on them, how can the love of God be in that person? Dear children, let us not love with words or speech but with actions and in truth."** Then he says in the next two verses, **"*This then is how we know that we belong to the truth*, and how we set our hearts at rest in his presence whenever our hearts condemn us"** (1 John 3:19-20, NIV1984). In other words, we can know we are genuine believers because we love our brothers and sisters in God's family and lay down our lives for them by loving them in very practical and sacrificial ways. So if you have a genuine and growing love for the family of God, or at least desire to have this, then you can be assured that you are genuinely saved and will make it to heaven.

The Holy Spirit

The last evidence of a genuine believer we will look at is found in 1 John 4:13, where John says, **"This is how we know that we live in him and he in us: *He has given us his Spirit.*"** John is saying here that we can have confidence that we are genuinely saved because God has given us the Holy Spirit. The apostle Paul says in Ephesians 1:13-14, **"And you also were included in Christ when you heard the message of truth, the gospel of your salvation.** *When you believed, you were marked in him with a seal, the promised Holy Spirit, who is a deposit guaranteeing our inheritance* **until the redemption of those who are God's possession—to the praise of his glory."** This means genuine believers, when they first believe the gospel, are given the Holy Spirit as a *guarantee* that they will inherit eternal life in heaven. The verse above says if you have the Holy Spirit, you are God's possession and are guaranteed a place in heaven. But the apostle Paul also says this in Romans 8:9: **"And if anyone does not have the Spirit of Christ, they do not belong to Christ."** Do you have the Holy Spirit living in you? If not, you do not belong to Christ and will not make it to heaven.

A genuine believer will have evidence in their lives that the Holy Spirit is living in them. What is that evidence? The description is found in Galatians 5:22-23 and is called *"the fruit of the Spirit,"* it says, **"But the fruit of the Spirit is love, joy, peace, patience, kindness, goodness, faithfulness, gentleness and self-control"** (NIV1984). These are the attributes the Holy Spirit produces in the life of a genuine believer; they are not produced by human effort, but by the power of the Holy Spirit and His working in the believer's life. Most people in the world have these to some degree, but in the life of a believer they should be more abundant, more consistent, and be growing in measure.

Before I got saved, I didn't have many of these *fruits* in my life. I probably had the opposite of them! However, after I got saved and received the Holy Spirit, He began to produce these things in my life more abundantly. I do not always have these *fruits* as much as I would like, but they are continually growing in my life and are evidence that I am saved, have the Holy Spirit living in me, and have a secure place in heaven.

In Romans 8:16, the apostle Paul says that, **"The Spirit himself testifies with our spirit that we are God's children."** If you are genuinely saved, the Holy Spirit lives in you and there will be evidence of this in your life. You will be developing, *"the fruit of the Spirit,"* as listed above and growing in godly character, and the Holy Spirit Himself will testify to you inwardly and outwardly that you are one of God's children. If you have evidence that the Holy Spirit lives in you, you can be certain that you will make it to heaven.

So how did you do? Do you have the marks of a true believer in your life? These are just a few of the indicators that someone should have in his or her life if he or she has been truly saved from their sin and born again. If you have these in your life you can have confidence and assurance that your faith is genuine, you have been saved, are truly born again, and will make it to heaven. Of course, if you are a recent or new believer in Jesus, these things may be very minimal in your life now, but they will continue to grow in you as you grow spiritually. The next chapter talks about steps you can take to grow spiritually and become a more mature believer.

Chapter 7

STEPS FOR GROWTH

When Jesus died on the cross for our sins, He did it not just so we could go to heaven when we die, but so we could be brought into a real and personal relationship with God here on earth. This is confirmed in 1 Peter 3:18: **"For Christ died for sins once for all, the righteousness for the unrighteous, *to bring you to God*"** (NIV1984). Jesus' death on the cross removes our sin and brings us back to God so we can have a relationship with Him. God wants to have a close relationship with us and He wants us to know Him. In John 17:3 Jesus says, **"Now this is eternal life: that they may *know you*, the only true God, and Jesus Christ, whom you have sent."** Receiving God's forgiveness and the free gift of eternal life is all about *knowing Him* and having a *relationship* with Him. It's not about being "religious" or doing religious things.

When you put your trust in Jesus to save you from your sins, it's only the beginning of a lifelong journey of getting to know Him better and walking in a daily relationship with Him. Like any relationship, there are certain steps we can take to strengthen and deepen our relationship with God, and that is the heart of this chapter.

If you have trusted Jesus as your Savior, you have been reborn spiritually and are just an infant in your new spiritual birth. There are certain steps you must take to grow strong and stay healthy. This chapter will give you five important steps you can take that will help strengthen your relationship with God and help you to mature and grow spiritually.

Find a Good Church

One of the first steps you must take to grow is to find a good church family and become a part of it. When you become born again by trusting Jesus as your Savior, you are born into the family of God. God is now your Father and other believers are now your brothers and sisters. There are several good reasons why God wants you to be a part of a church family; one being, He wants you to have close relationships with other members of your new spiritual family. You will need these relationships with other believers to receive encouragement and grow in your faith. In Hebrews 10:25 it says, **"Let us not give up meeting together, as some are in the habit of doing, but let us encourage one another—and all the more as you see the Day approaching"** (NIV1984). God wants you to meet regularly with other believers so you can be encouraged in your faith and so you can encourage others.

Another good reason for being part of a church family is so that you can receive solid teaching from God's Word. There are many churches out there to choose from, but good ones believe the Bible is God's inspired Word from cover to cover. A good church will teach you the Word of God and help you to understand it better. If you are currently involved in a church and realize they are not really helping you know and understand God's Word better, you may want to visit some other churches in your area and find one that does. This process may be a bit uncomfortable, especially if you have been in the same church all your life, but you need to get out of your comfort zone (and perhaps your tradition), visit some other churches, and find one that will actually encourage you in your faith and teach you the Word of God. Have some fun with this. It can be a kind of an adventure for you. However, be patient, as it may take some time before you find the right church for you.

Becoming part of a good church is a must if you want to grow in your faith.

**"A good church will teach you the Word of God and
help you to understand it better."**

Get Baptized

Once you get established in a good church family, another step you must take to grow in your faith is to be baptized. The word *baptize* means, "to immerse" or "submerge." Jesus commanded all those who believed the good news about Him to be baptized or immersed in water. Baptism was to be a public declaration that you have trusted Jesus as your Savior and that you are now following Him as the Lord of your life. Baptism is also kind of like a funeral service for the old you. When you trust Jesus as your Savior, the old you dies and needs to be buried. So when your whole body is immersed under the water, it is a picture of burying the old you and your old life. When you come up out of the water, it is a picture of you being resurrected to a new life—from being spiritually dead to being spiritually alive. Baptism doesn't accomplish these things, but is a picture of what has already happened to you the moment you put your faith in Jesus.

Remember that baptism does not wash away your sins or have anything to do with getting you into heaven. If you have put your faith in the sacrifice of Jesus Christ, your sins are already washed away and you have the promise of eternal life in heaven. Remember the one thief who was crucified with Jesus? He was never baptized, but on the cross he put his faith in Jesus as his Savior. Jesus promised that he would be with Him in paradise that very day. So you won't go to hell if you don't get baptized, but it was important enough that Jesus commanded His followers to be baptized.

If you were baptized as an infant, you need to know that the Scriptures never give a command to baptize babies because baptism is for those who understand and believe the gospel; it is for those who have made a decision to trust Jesus as their Savior—something impossible for infants to do. It was also to be the personal choice of the believer once they have been born again. In infant baptism, parents or guardians make the choice, not the baby. So I would encourage you, once you have trusted Jesus as your Savior and have found a good church family to plug into, talk to the pastor about taking the next step in your faith and obey the Lord's command to be baptized (even if you were baptized as an infant).

Read the Bible

Another vital step you must take to start growing in your faith is to read the Bible. The Bible has many different functions in the life of a believer and we will look briefly at just a few of them. One of the functions of the Bible is simply to help us *know God better*. The Bible teaches us who God is, what He is like, what He has done for us, and how He expects us to live and relate to Him.

Another function of God's Word in the life of a believer is to give us *spiritual nourishment.* The apostle Peter, describing the Word of God as our spiritual milk, says, **"Like newborn babies, crave pure spiritual milk, so that by it you may grow up in your salvation"** (1 Peter 2:2). Peter is calling believers to crave the Word of God just as newborn babies crave milk, because it will help us to grow up spiritually and become strong in our faith. When Jesus was in the desert being tempted by Satan to turn stone into bread, He responded to Satan saying, **"Man does not live on bread alone, but on every word that comes from the mouth of God"** (Matthew 4:4, NIV1984). Jesus was saying that God's Word is like spiritual bread to us; it sustains us and gives us our spiritual strength and energy. Imagine if you went without food for a week or more. How would you feel? You would probably feel tired and weak. It will be the same if we neglect reading and feeding on God's Word—we will become spiritually tired, weak, and we won't grow as God wants us to grow.

The Bible also functions to *equip believers* to do good works and live lives that are pleasing to God. Second Timothy 3:16-17 says: **"All Scripture is God-breathed and is useful for *teaching*, *rebuking*, *correcting* and *training in righteousness*, so that the servant of God may be thoroughly equipped for every good work."** So we need God's Word because it teaches us, rebukes us, corrects us, and trains us in righteousness, so we are prepared to do everything that God calls us to do in life.

The Bible also reveals that God's Word acts like a sword—a *spiritual weapon* for believers against Satan and his demons. In Ephesians 6:17, the Word of God is called, **"the sword of the Spirit."** In Matthew chapter 4, when Jesus was being tempted by Satan, we see that Jesus defeated Satan's temptations by quoting the Word of God to him. Like Jesus, we need the Word of God to fight against Satan's temptations and lies that come against us every day.

". . . we need the Word of God to fight against Satan's temptations and lies that come against us every day."

If you don't yet have a Bible, you can get one at your local Christian bookstore or just about any bookstore (even many local department stores carry them), or order one online. There are also many Bible apps you can download to your smartphone, tablet, or mp3 player. There are many different translations or versions of the Bible, but all say the same thing, just in a different way. Some use more modern English words and some use English words that are a bit older.

If you are new to Bible reading, I suggest either the New International Version (NIV) or the New Living Translation (NLT). When you start reading the Bible, I also suggest you *not* start at the beginning, in the book of Genesis. That may sound kind of strange, but the Bible is not like any other book, it is actually one book composed of sixty-six different "books" or "letters." The Bible is also divided into two main sections: the "Old Testament," which covers the time before Jesus was on earth, and the "New Testament," which covers the lifetime of Jesus and His apostles. I suggest you go to the *Gospel of John* in the New Testament, and start reading there. If you want some extra help in understanding the Bible, you may consider buying a "study Bible." These contain extra notes that will help explain or give special insight into the Bible verses and passages you read. You can also find many helpful resources online or on downloadable apps. You can try looking up "Bible Commentaries." These will allow you to look up certain passages of Scripture and read comments from Bible scholars who explain a little more about each particular Bible verse.

Be patient as you begin reading your Bible. Some of what you read may seem hard to understand, or even confusing. However, the more you read and study it, the better you will understand it. Once again, it will also be very helpful for you to be part of a church that actually teaches you how to understand the Bible.

Prayer

Another important step you must take to start growing in your faith is to pray. Prayer is simply talking to God. God talks to us through His Word and through the Holy Spirit, and we talk to God through prayer. If we want any relationship to be closer and stronger, it requires time spent together and heart-to-heart communication. This is no different in your relationship with God. If you want your relationship with God to be closer and stronger, you need to spend time alone with Him; listening to Him through His Word, and talking to Him through prayer.

"If we want any relationship to be closer and stronger, it requires time spent together and heart-to-heart communication. This is no different in your relationship with God."

Prayer is not just repeating a pre-written prayer—that's not what God wants from you. He wants to hear from *you*, from your own heart, in your own words. In communicating my love to my wife, she doesn't want me to just repeat words that someone else has written, she wants to hear words that come from *my* heart. Repeating a pre-written prayer is kind of like giving my wife a Valentine's Day card with someone else's thoughts and words on it and just signing my name to it—it's not a very sufficient or genuine way of communicating my love to her. In that card, I should write something that comes from my own heart to express my genuine love to my wife.

Jesus rebuked the most religious people of His day by quoting these words from Isaiah the prophet: **"These people honor me with their lips, but their hearts are far from me"** (Matthew 15:8). Jesus doesn't want your prayers to just be repeated words coming from your lips, but words that come from your heart.

The "Our Father" (or "Lord's Prayer") and all other pre-written prayers were never meant for us to simply repeat with our lips. They must be prayed from the heart. Can they be repeated and come from the heart? Yes. However, it is difficult to repeat prayers without them becoming mere habits or rituals. The "Lord's Prayer" was meant to be a model for prayer or things that should be contained in our prayers: praise to God, praying for God's Kingdom, for God's will to be done, asking God to meet our daily needs, confessing our sins, forgiving those who have sinned against us, asking God for protection against temptation and the devil.

Finally, prayer is something that grows and develops with time and use. The Bible has much to say about prayer and will teach you how to pray. So, as you take the time to pray, read God's Word, and develop your relationship with God, you will learn better how to pray and communicate with God.

Sharing the Good News

The last important step I want to share with you for growing in your faith is that of sharing the gospel or good news of Jesus with others. Jesus actually gave us this as a command in Mark 16:15:

"He said to them, 'Go into all the world and preach the good news to all creation'" (NIV1984). When I first came to hear and understand how to make it to heaven, I realized that all my life I mistakenly thought I would go to heaven when I died. In reality, if I had died back then, before trusting Jesus as my Savior, I would have ended up in hell for all eternity, with no chance or hope of ever getting out.

For me, that was a frightening thought! It was a wake-up call! I began to think about all the people I knew—even strangers—who were in the same place I was, mistakenly thinking they will make it to heaven someday because of their own goodness, good deeds, or religious works. I began to think about their eternal destiny and where they would end up if they didn't repent and trust Jesus as their Savior. I had a real burden and desire to share this message with others. So one of the first things I did was take a class at my church on how to share the gospel with others.

You may not have a class at your church that will teach you how to share the gospel, but there are plenty of books and online courses that can help you out. Just type *evangelism training* into your online search engine and you will find plenty of resources to help you out. *Evangelism* simply means sharing the gospel or good news about Jesus Christ. I highly recommend going to the website *livingwaters.com.* It offers some great training resources that will teach you how to share the gospel in an easy, effective, and understandable way. They also carry many gospel "tracts"; little publications you can buy that contain the gospel message. You can simply give them to people when you don't have time to talk, are too scared, or just don't know what to say.

Think for a moment of all the people you know who believe they are going to end up in heaven because they believe they are good. They are relying on themselves, their good deeds, or religious works to get to heaven. Think of all the people you know who are not born again or saved by putting their trust in Jesus alone. Please don't be fooled into thinking: "Oh, they will be okay.

God wouldn't send them to hell. They believe in Jesus. They go to church. They do a lot of good things and are pretty good overall." (If you still believe that someone will enter heaven because they are good or because of anything other than relying on Jesus and His death on the cross, then you have missed the whole point of this book and need to go back and read it again.) Think about their Judgment Day when they will hear Jesus say to them, **"I never knew you. Away from me, you evildoers!"** (Matthew 7:23). Think about them spending eternity in hell, with no chance of ever getting out. Now what are you going to do about it? Well, first of all you can begin to pray for them; pray that they will come to discover the truth of how to make it to heaven. You could also simply pass along a copy of this book to them.

I have shared this message with many people over the years and I have seen many people trust Jesus as their Savior. This book is just another way I am trying to reach people with the good news of Jesus Christ. Think for a moment of all the things in life that are important to you. Think of all the things you spend your time and money on. Now, think about eternity. Of all these things, what will matter in eternity? What will last? There is only one thing we can take with us into heaven, and that is other people. They can only make it if they hear the good news about Jesus and make the decision to rely on His sacrifice alone for the forgiveness of their sins. So, the most important thing we can do in this life—the best use of our time and money—is to do all we can to share with as many people as we can how they can make it to heaven. So begin to do something today. Help others make it to heaven, before it's too late.

NOTES

[1] Charles Darwin, *On the Origin of Species* (London: J. M. Dent & Sons Ltd., 1971), p. 167.
[2] Robert Jastrow, "Evolution: Selection for perfection," *Science Digest*, December 1981, p. 86.